Thrive in a Changing Economy: Alternative Careers for a Sustainable Future.

How to Pursue and Excel in High-Demand Green Careers Without a Formal Degree.

Copyright Jonathan Frost © 2023

The right of Jonathan Frost to be identified as the author of this work has been asserted in accordance with the copyright designs and patent Act 1988

drjonathanfrost.com

ISBN: 9798867778699

Imprint: Independently published

All rights reserved. No part of this publication may be reproduced, stored in a retrieval system or transmitted in any form or by any means electronic, mechanical, photocopying, recording and/or otherwise without the prior written permission of the publishers. This book may not be lent, resold, hired out or otherwise disposed of by way of trading any form, binding or cover other than that in which it is published without the prior consent of the publishers.

Printed by Amazon

Table of Contents

Preface 1

1: Challenge the Traditional Path 4

2: Soar As A Solar Panel Installer 15

3: The Rise Of Wind Turbine Technicians 24

4: Community Gardeners And Urban Farmers 33

5: Resplendent Recycling Centre Operators 48

6: Vital Water Harvesting Technicians 60

7: Triumph In The Bicycle Repair Industry 74

8: High Demand For Home Retrofitting Experts 86

9: Conquer The Art of Composting 97

10: Bloom Off The Beaten Track 111

Acknowledgements

I am happy and proud to acknowledge help and encouragement from Sean Vosler and the team at Movable Type.

Dedication

To My Growing Family, Lorraine, Peter, Ben, Grace, Jodie, Jay, Emma, Ruben and Elora

Preface

"Change is the law of life. And those who look only to the past or present are certain to miss the future."

- John F. Kennedy

If you are holding this book, consider it as a ticket to a thrilling expedition to explore careers that chart a journey less travelled. Is it possible to have an empowering career without a formal degree? Through this book, we will respond with a resounding 'yes'! In your hands, lies a comprehensive roadmap for alternative careers that tap into the elements of a sustainable future and a rapidly changing economy.

I've crafted this book with you in mind - young individuals interested in a meaningful career that goes beyond the confines of traditional degrees. I want to debunk the myth that viable and sustainable career options are found only after several years spent in formal education. Poised to burst that bubble, this book introduces you to versatile, sustainable, and high-in-demand careers that don't require a conventional diploma.

At some point, I, too, was in your shoes. A bright-eyed young individual, curious about picking a path less crowded, yet profitable. Stories of people like us, who've dared to dream and think differently, ultimately nudging the world to change its course of thought over time, inspired me to write this book. I began this journey into uncharted waters when I met Sarah, a young woman who chose to be a sustainable energy consultant instead of following the much worn MBA route. Sarah's trailblazing journey led me to Alex, a self-taught programmer who now heads an AI startup. Weaving together these tales from the trenches, this book takes form to help you set your own bearings and a course that suits you.

I thank many mentors, colleagues, and field experts for the inputs that lent critical insights to this endeavour. My appreciation extends to these change-makers who shared their professional journeys, personal highs, and lows to weave a narrative for what the 21st-century global job market holds for non-degree holders. Their enchanting tales are the lifeblood of this book, intended to provide both inspiration and actionable insights for you.

As the reader, you're the reason this book exists. I appreciate the time you invest in understanding the information and insights that unfold page by page. You 'could' have been anywhere doing anything else, yet you chose to inquire, to learn, to prepare for an alternative career with enthusiasm. Your curiosity and desire to redefine success are commendable.

An open mind, curiosity to learn, and a willingness to explore new opportunities, that's all you need to ignite the spark within you. This book is meticulously designed for young, proactive individuals and aspirants who are seeking a path full of potential that co-exists with sustainable economic development.

I'm utterly thankful that you have chosen this conduit to inform, enlighten, and perhaps, transform your career trajectory. Keep going, and I promise, by the time you flip the last page, you'll be equipped with the practical knowledge to chart your own course.

Now, isn't it time to step into the future boldly?

Welcome on board and let this discovery of alternative careers begin!

Remember, the future belongs to those who believe in the beauty of their dreams.

1: Challenge the Traditional Path

A green economy begins to replace some of the clunking and chugging of ugly machines with the wise effort of beautiful, skilled people. That means more jobs.

Van Jones

In the shadows of the vibrant, bustling social hub known as the local 'Suited Crowd Club,' the figure of Jim Muldoon could be seen, heavy laden with thoughts. This energetic locale was the beating heart of the small town, almost a Mecca for bright-eyed, newly graduated townsfolk positively bursting with their fresh diplomas and job designations. The club hummed with music, laughter, and youth; their tales of triumph weaving together over frothy pints. But within that joyful buzz, Jim sensed an invisible spectre, a silent rule of society: that success was invariably tied to academic achievements.

Jim found himself a frequent visitor to the Suited Crowd Club, his thoughts oscillating between embracing the beaten path and resisting it. He didn't fit within the crisp, university-educated pattern of the club patrons. Instead, his memories echoed with the comforting melody of power saws in his grandfather's old woodworking shop. He revelled in the rustic aroma of fresh timber and cherished the wisdom passed down from the seasoned craftsmen navigating him through his apprenticeship experience. His artistic creation of empowering and impactful objects through carpentry indeed brought him joy. This satisfaction, however, often found itself clouded by an undesired question: why hadn't he sought a formal degree like his peers?

One evening, as he departed from the Suited Crowd Club, the atmosphere hung heavy with his internal debates. The golden sun was pulling down a velvet blanket upon the town's simple beauty while distant whiffs of fuel from the local airstrip teased his senses. Breathing in the mechanical scent juxtaposed against nature's calm, Jim had an epiphany. Much like the daily cycle of sunrise and sunset, societal norms keep changing.

Without a traditional degree, Jim appreciated that he was the master of his own existence; his blueprint wasn't sketched inside lecture halls. His craft was a journey shaped out of tactile manipulation, hard work, and experience. He bore no scholarly badges of honour, nor was he robed in any academic gown. Instead, his attire told a story of countless hours spent under watchful elders, his palms marked with the calluses earned through the mastery of his trade.

Despite those ardent reflections, the haunting question lingered on in his mind—did his education or rather, lack thereof, define his worth or limit his potential? As he succumbed towards slumber later that evening, the solemn twinkling stars seemed to underscore his silent quandaries. Would society ever evolve to validate that success could be sowed and reaped outside academic pastures? Could it ever recognize that passion, hands-on experience, and unwavering dedication rivalled a traditional degree's worth?

Challenging the Traditional Path: Alternative Careers for a Sustainable Future

In the ever-changing landscape of the economy, it's becoming increasingly clear that the traditional path to success is no longer the only option. The days of believing that a formal degree is the only route to a fulfilling and well-paid career are slowly fading away. Instead, a new paradigm is emerging - one that emphasises practical experience, specialised training, and a willingness to challenge the status quo.

This chapter, the first of the book "Thrive in a Changing Economy: Alternative Careers for a Sustainable Future," is dedicated to exploring the world of alternative careers that don't require a formal degree. We will delve into the many opportunities that exist in fields that will grow in importance and demand as resources become scarce, and we will challenge the conventional belief that a degree is the ultimate prerequisite for success.

Many high-demand careers today don't necessarily require the traditional four-year degree. Instead, they may require some form of training, apprenticeship, or hands-on experience. By challenging the notion that a degree is a prerequisite for success, we open up a world of possibilities for individuals who may not have pursued higher education but possess the drive and passion to excel in their chosen field.

In this chapter, we will explore a multitude of alternative pathways to career success, each requiring specialised skills and knowledge rather than a formal degree. From renewable energy technicians and sustainable agriculture specialists to cybersecurity experts and data scientists, these alternative careers offer abundant opportunities for growth and success. Each profession will be presented in detail, outlining the specific training and hands-on experience required, as well as the potential growth and demand in the field.

By introducing these alternative careers, we hope to provide a fresh perspective on how to thrive in a changing economy. We want to empower individuals who may feel constrained by the traditional education system and offer them hope and inspiration for a future where formal degrees are not the only measure of success. Our aim is to equip our readers with the knowledge and tools they need to explore and pursue these alternative careers, unleashing their full potential in a sustainable and prosperous future.

Let's embark on this exciting adventure together. Let's challenge the traditional path, explore alternative careers, and unleash our true potential in a changing economy.

Imagine taking a different path, one that allows you to pursue a career that aligns with your passions and values. Now, I know what you might be thinking – how is this possible without a degree? Well, that's precisely what we're about to explore together.

Many industries are evolving and shifting in response to changing economic and environmental conditions. As resources become scarce, certain careers will grow in importance and demand. These careers generally don't necessitate a full-fledged degree, but instead prioritise practical experience and specialised training.

Think of it like embarking on a new adventure, where every step along the way brings you closer to a meaningful and fulfilling career. Just like a treasure map, this book will guide you through alternative careers that don't require a formal degree. Each career represents a unique opportunity for you to thrive in a changing economy and contribute to sustainable practices in your chosen field.

Let's set sail and explore these alternative pathways to career success. By challenging the traditional path and expanding our mindset, we can unlock a world of possibilities. It's time to liberate ourselves from the confines of societal norms and discover the breadth of opportunities available. It won't always be easy, but with the right mindset and guidance, we can forge our own path to success.

Now, you might be wondering what separates these alternative careers from the traditional ones that often require a four-year degree. The key lies in the emphasis on practical experience and specialised training. Instead of spending years in classrooms studying theories, you'll have the opportunity to jump right into the field and gain hands-on experience.

This approach allows for quicker entry into the workforce and creates a seamless transition between learning and doing. By immersing yourself in real-world scenarios from the start, you'll develop the skills and knowledge necessary to excel in your chosen career.

But don't worry – this doesn't mean you'll be left to navigate this path alone. Throughout this journey, you'll discover the resources and support systems available to guide you along the way. Whether it's through apprenticeships, mentorship programs, or specialised training courses, you'll find the tools you need to succeed.

Are you ready to challenge the status quo? To pave your own way to success? Then let's continue our exploration of alternative careers and uncover the exciting possibilities that lie ahead. So, grab a compass and join me as we navigate the uncharted waters of the future. Together, we can create a world where success is defined by passion, purpose, and practical experience.

There is an African proverb that says: "If you want to go fast, go alone, if you want to go far, go together."

Challenge the Conventional Belief That a Formal Degree is a Prerequisite for Success in High-Demand Careers

In our society, there is a prevailing belief that higher education and a formal degree are the only paths to success. We are told from a young age that we must go to college, earn a degree, and then we will have access to high-paying, stable careers. Traditional parents used to have this kind of belief system. But is this really true now? Are there no other paths to success?

The reality is, there are many high-demand careers that don't require a formal degree. This may come as a surprise to some, but it is an important truth that we need to challenge. It is time to question the conventional belief that a degree is the only path to success.

Think about it this way: imagine you are about to embark on a journey to a new destination. You have a map that shows the traditional route that everyone takes, but you also have access to alternative routes that may be faster, more scenic, or less congested. Would you blindly follow the traditional route because everyone else is doing it, or would you consider the alternatives?

Just like in our metaphorical journey, there are alternative paths to success in your career. These paths may require different skills, training, or experiences, but they can lead you to the same destination. By challenging the conventional belief that a formal degree is the only way to succeed, you open yourself up to a world of possibilities.

Let's take a moment to explore some alternative paths that lead to successful, high-demand careers. Imagine you are standing at a crossroads, surrounded by different signs pointing in different directions. One sign leads to a career in renewable energy, another to sustainable agriculture, and yet another to digital marketing. Each of these paths requires specialised skills and knowledge, but none of them require a formal degree.

By challenging the conventional belief about the necessity of a degree, you are empowering yourself to pursue a career that aligns with your passions and interests, rather than feeling constrained by the traditional path. You are giving yourself the freedom to explore different options and find a career that fulfils you in ways that a degree alone cannot. A degree is just a piece of paper. Whilst it is generally believed that knowledge is the key to success, it is not always true. Practical experiences serve as a key to success too.

So next time someone tells you that you need a degree to succeed, remember that there are alternative paths to success. Challenge the conventional belief, explore different options, and pave your own way to a fulfilling and rewarding career. Don't be afraid to take the road less travelled – you might just find that it leads you to exactly where you want to be.

Thrive in a Changing Economy

Explore alternative pathways to career success that emphasise practical experience and specialised training.

In today's rapidly changing economy, the traditional path to career success is no longer the only option. The notion that a formal degree is a prerequisite for success is being challenged, as many high-demand careers actually value practical experience and specialised training more than a diploma. This is good news for those who may not have pursued higher education, but it also means that they need to explore alternative pathways to reach their career goals.

Rather than being limited by a lack of a degree, individuals can embrace their unique skills and passions and seek out careers that align with their interests. By focusing on practical experience and specialised training, they can develop the necessary expertise to thrive in a changing economy. These alternative pathways often provide a faster and more direct route to success, bypassing the traditional academic route.

It's important to note that these alternative pathways are not shortcuts or easy routes to success. They require hard work, dedication, and a commitment to continuous learning. However, for those who are willing to put in the effort, they offer a viable and fulfilling alternative to the traditional career path.

One alternative pathway is through apprenticeships or on-the-job training programs. These programs allow individuals to learn and develop skills while working alongside experienced professionals. This hands-on experience not only provides valuable training but also allows for networking and industry connections.

Apprenticeships can be found in a range of fields, from construction and manufacturing to healthcare and IT.

Another option is to pursue vocational training or certifications in specific industries or fields. These programs offer specialised training and education that equip individuals with the practical skills needed for success in their chosen careers. For example, someone interested in the renewable energy sector could pursue a certification in solar panel installation or wind turbine maintenance. These specialised skills are in high demand as the world transitions to more sustainable energy sources.

In addition to vocational training, there are also online courses and resources available that allow individuals to learn and develop new skills at their own pace. These online platforms offer a wide range of subjects and topics, making it possible for individuals to gain the knowledge they need to excel in their chosen field. This flexibility is especially beneficial for those who may already be working or have other commitments that make attending traditional classes difficult. Today, online courses and platforms seem to be a convenient tool for people to learn at their own pace.

By exploring these alternative pathways and embracing practical experience and specialised training, individuals can find fulfilling and sustainable careers without the need for a formal degree. The key is to identify the skills and industries that align with their interests and invest in their own professional development. With determination and a willingness to learn, success is within reach, no matter the educational background. So, don't let the lack of a degree hold you back. Embrace the alternative pathways to career success and thrive in a changing economy.

Alternative Careers: Breaking Free from the Mould

Thrive in a Changing Economy

First and foremost, we must discard the notion that a formal degree is an absolute prerequisite for a successful career. In fact, many highly sought-after professions thrive on practical experience and specialised training. Just think about it... some of the most successful people in the world didn't follow the traditional academic route. They sought out hands-on experience, honed their skills, and ventured into uncharted territory. They dared to challenge the status quo and carved their own paths to success.

Opening Our Eyes to New Possibilities

By exploring alternative pathways, we open a world of fresh opportunities. It's like stepping into a vibrant marketplace, filled with niche careers that cater to the demands of our changing economy. As resources become increasingly scarce, professionals who possess the skills to navigate this new landscape will be in high-demand. But the best part? These careers don't necessarily require the comprehensive education that traditional jobs demand. Instead, they require a different kind of education - one that emphasises apprenticeships, specialised training, and hands-on experience.

Thriving in a Sustainable Future

Imagine a future where we thrive on renewable energy, sustainable agriculture, and cutting-edge technology that safeguards our environment. By embracing alternative careers, we can contribute to this future. We become architects of change, driving progress in areas such as renewable energy, conservation, sustainable farming, and green building. We can build a world where success is defined not only by financial gain but also by the positive impact we make on our planet.

Igniting a Passion for Lifelong Learning

By pursuing alternative careers, we recognize the importance of lifelong learning. We discard the notion that education ends with a formal degree. Instead, we embrace a culture of curiosity and continuous growth. We understand that knowledge is not locked away in textbooks but is waiting to be discovered through hands-on experience and specialised training. And as we immerse ourselves in these practical pursuits, we unlock the boundless potential within us. Learning is a life-long journey. There is so much potential inside us rather than just merely relying on textbooks.

Embracing the Journey Ahead

As we conclude this chapter, I want to remind you that there is an abundance of alternative pathways to career success that await you. Open your mind to the possibilities that lie outside the confines of traditional education. Embrace the idea that success is not limited to those who hold degrees but is attainable for anyone willing to invest their time and dedication.

So, take a deep breath, and let the excitement for the future wash over you. The chapters that lay ahead will unveil fifteen alternative careers that are not only in high demand but will also play a crucial role in shaping a sustainable future. Get ready to dive into the fascinating world of renewable energy, sustainable agriculture, conservation, and so much more. The journey ahead is filled with possibilities, and I am thrilled to be walking it with you.

2: Soar As A Solar Panel Installer

The future is green energy, sustainability, renewable energy.

Arnold Schwarzenegger

Picture the idyllic expanse of Kansas—a sea of wheat fields bathed in golden sunlight, undulating endlessly under an impossibly wide sky. Here in this pastoral paradise, Braden Walsh, a tradesman gifted with the delicate task of installing solar panels, greets the day at sunrise. The morning is tranquil—a perfect, still setting where the cool air embraces Bradley's determination and the earth itself seems to anticipate the new day's first light. All around, silence prevails, interrupted only by the gentle whisper of crops swaying.

Having apprenticed under his father at Walsh & Sons, Braden has been a beacon for the renewable energy revolution since childhood. Braden's father, an electrical engineer who found his second calling advocating for renewable energy, became animated when speaking of harvesting sunlight's power. Braden soaked up that fervour as if he were one of the absorbent silicon cells he now handled; his hands were the loving guardians of a more sustainable future.

The crunch of work boots on gravel marks Braden's path to the barn—now a makeshift storage loft filled with rows upon rows of solar panels looking like mirrors reflecting back the open, blue sky.

Thrive in a Changing Economy

Each mirror glows with the tranquil promise of a revolution drawn out from the sun's rays. Installing panel after panel with his father, they each matched their spanner turns to the thrumming beat of conviction in their veins. Their craft extended beyond mere breadwinning—it was a means for every household to harness sun-given energy, to distance themselves from pitiless power giants and take up a stake in preserving our precious world.

Yet, even as purposeful as his work was, it demanded from Braden a monumental depth of understanding about electrical systems. Every time he fit a panel in place on a rooftop, it felt like untangling intricate riddles: where should optimal placement be for ideal sunlight access? What pitch should panels sit at for peak solar absorption? Who was best served by which inverter model fitting their home's individual layout and energy requirements? And of course, all this discernment needed to be exercised under the relentless tutelage of the sun—ever-present, unyielding and open handed.

Midday sunlight weighs heavy on Braden as he unloads panels from his truck, the currencies of his trade. A shadow of unease creeps over him despite the bright surroundings. Change was afoot; he could feel it in the collective voice rallying behind renewable energy. But change also roared its ominous growl; the old energy regime's shadow seemed to stretch far and ominously over his ambition. It left him uncertain—would the sweat shed under this searing Kansas sun truly usher forth a new age? Or would the petroleum-touting titans continue to consume Earth's dwindling resources unchecked? By adopting a profession in solar power, has he correctly anticipated the surging wave of green energy? Or is he simply tilting at windmills under an endless Kansas sky?

The Growing Demand for Solar Panel Installers: Riding the Wave of Renewable Energy

Welcome to Chapter 2 of "Thrive in a Changing Economy: Alternative Careers for a Sustainable Future"! In this chapter, we will delve into the exciting world of renewable energy and explore one of the most in-demand careers in this field: solar panel installation. As society increasingly shifts towards clean energy sources like solar power, the need for skilled technicians to install and maintain solar panels will continue to rise.

1. Recognize the growing demand for renewable energy and its impact on the need for solar panel installers.

Renewable energy is no longer just a buzzword; it is now a driving force in our changing economy. The mounting concerns over climate change, the depletion of fossil fuels, and rising energy costs have prompted a widespread shift towards sustainable energy solutions. Solar power, in particular, has emerged as a frontrunner in the race to a more sustainable future. As a result, there is a growing demand for solar panel installers who can help harness the power of the sun and convert it into clean, reliable electricity.

2. Understand the role and responsibilities of solar panel installers in the renewable energy industry.

Imagine standing on the roof of a house, securing solar panels under the warm glow of the sun. As a solar panel installer, that could be your reality. Your primary responsibility as a solar panel installer is to mount solar panels on rooftops or ground-mounted systems to capture sunlight and generate electricity. This may sound simple, but the work requires a keen eye for detail, as each panel must be securely fastened, correctly angled, and connected to the electrical system of the building. You will also need to conduct regular maintenance and troubleshoot any issues to ensure the panels are working efficiently.

3. Learn about the training and skills required to pursue a career as a solar panel installer.

While a formal degree is not always necessary, you do need to acquire a specific set of skills to excel in this field. First and foremost, a solid foundation in electrical concepts is crucial. As a solar panel installer, you will be working with high-voltage DC circuits, wiring, and electrical components, so understanding the principles of electricity is essential. Additionally, you will need practical skills such as how to safely use tools, interpret technical diagrams, and follow installation instructions. Moreover, staying updated with the latest industry standards and regulations through certifications and training programs is vital in this ever-evolving field.

Now that we have delved into the three key items you will learn in this chapter, it is crucial to underscore the significance of pursuing a career as a solar panel installer in our changing economy. By becoming a part of the renewable energy revolution, you will not only contribute to a more sustainable future but also enjoy a wide range of benefits, including job security, competitive salaries, and personal satisfaction from making a positive impact on the world.

So, join us as we soar above and uncover the opportunities that await those who are ready to embrace the demand for solar panel installers. In the following sections, we will explore the various aspects of this career path, including the benefits, challenges, and tips for success. Whether you are starting from scratch or looking to transition into a more sustainable career, this chapter will equip you with the knowledge and inspiration you need to thrive as a solar panel installer in a changing economy. Let's get started!

Framework: The STEPS Model for Solar Panel Installers
Introducing the STEPS Model: a comprehensive framework that outlines the training and skills required to pursue a career as a solar panel installer. This model will serve as your guide as you embark on this exciting and impactful journey into the renewable energy industry.

Skills

The first component of the STEPS Model is Skills. As a solar panel installer, you will need to possess a range of technical skills to effectively install and maintain solar panels. These skills include electrical knowledge, familiarity with building codes and regulations, and the ability to troubleshoot and solve problems. Additionally, you will need strong communication skills to effectively interact with clients and team members, as well as organisational skills to manage projects and coordinate installations.

Training

The second component of the STEPS Model is Training. Formal education is not always required to become a solar panel installer, but the necessary training and certifications will greatly enhance your credibility and employability. Training programs offered by industry associations, vocational schools, or community colleges can provide you with the knowledge and skills needed to succeed in this field. These programs typically cover topics such as solar technology, electrical systems, working at height safety protocols, and installation techniques.

Experience

The third component of the STEPS Model is Experience. Gaining hands-on experience in solar panel installation is crucial for becoming a competent and confident installer. Seek opportunities to work as an apprentice or gain practical experience through internships or entry-level positions. Additionally, consider volunteering for community projects or pursuing side projects to build your portfolio and demonstrate your capabilities. Working on any build project is a good start.

Professional Network

The fourth component of the STEPS Model is a Professional Network. Building a strong network of industry professionals is key to advancing your career as a solar panel installer. Join industry associations, attend conferences and workshops, and connect with like-minded individuals in the field. Not only will this help you stay updated on the latest industry trends and technologies, but it will also open doors for potential job opportunities and collaborations. Remember to keep in touch with local bricks and mortar businesses.

Soft Skills

The fifth component of the STEPS Model is Soft Skills. In addition to technical skills, employers value solar panel installers who possess strong soft skills. These include effective communication, teamwork, problem-solving, and customer service skills.

Demonstrating your ability to work well with others and meet the needs of clients will set you apart and lead to long-term success in the field.

The STEPS Model provides a holistic view of the training and skills required to excel as a solar panel installer. By focusing on each component of this framework, you will be well-equipped to pursue a rewarding career in the renewable energy industry. Remember, this is not just a job, but a chance to contribute to a more sustainable future and make a positive impact on the world around you.

The Future of Solar Panel Installers

As we conclude this chapter, it is clear that the demand for solar panel installers is set to soar to new heights. The world is waking up to the urgent need for clean, renewable energy, and solar power is leading the way. **The sun, with its boundless energy, has become a beacon of hope for a sustainable future.** And as more and more individuals, businesses, and governments make the switch to solar, the need for skilled installers will only continue to grow.

Think about it for a moment. **Every solar panel installed is a small step towards a greener planet**, a step away from our dependence on fossil fuels and the catastrophic consequences they bring. It is a tangible contribution towards reducing carbon emissions and combatting climate change.

Now, let's take a closer look at what it means to be a solar panel installer. They are the unsung heroes of the renewable energy revolution, the hands that bring solar power to life. These technicians are the ones who climb rooftops, face the elements, and ensure that the panels are installed correctly, efficiently, and safely. From planning the layout to mounting the panels to wiring the system, they are responsible for every step of the installation process. Their hard work and expertise are what make solar power a reality for so many.

Like in any job, a strong **work ethic** is a non-negotiable requirement for anyone considering a career in solar panel installation. This field demands physical labour, often in challenging weather conditions. It takes determination, perseverance, and a willingness to get the job done, no matter the obstacles. **If you're the kind of person who thrives on hard work and takes pride in a job well done, then you already possess a key ingredient for success.**

Another important trait is **attention to detail**. As a solar panel installer, you will be working with precision equipment and dealing with electrical systems. One small mistake can have significant consequences. **The ability to carefully follow instructions and double-check your work is critical to ensuring the safety and performance of the solar energy system.**

But don't worry if you don't have a background in electrical or construction work. **What matters most is a willingness to learn and adapt.** Many training programs and apprenticeships are available to help aspiring installers gain the necessary skills and knowledge. These programs often combine classroom instruction with hands-on experience, giving you the opportunity to learn from seasoned professionals in the field.

So, if you have a passion for renewable energy, a strong work ethic, and a desire to make a positive impact on the world, a career as a solar panel installer may be just what you're looking for. As the demand for clean energy continues to grow, so too will the need for skilled technicians who can bring solar power to life. **So, let's soar above the horizon together, bringing the power of the sun to every corner of the planet.**

3: The Rise Of Wind Turbine Technicians

Being green and clean is not just an aspiration but an action.

Christine Pelosi

Out on the vast Kansas plain, John D'Amico faced the unyielding gusts, each breath in his lungs laced with the taste of metal and unchartered freedom. He stood dwarfed by the giant wind turbine steel tower whose silhouette was a bold statement of progress.

D'Amico's journey to becoming a wind turbine technician was never paved by the traditional edifice of academia. Instead, it was through relentless hands-on work and immersion that he gleaned his education. He nurtured an intimate knowledge of the turbine's constitution – from each bolt to relay, from each safety killswitch to pivot point, tuning himself to their sanguine symphony of hums and whirrs. Touched by the rise in renewable wind power, his once agrarian native landscape sprung new life. Wind energy had invigorated the ageing heart of D'Amico too—it was bigger than routine—it gave him purpose.

As the day ebbed on, D'Amico envisioned an army of individuals eager to pursue a life like his in this clean energy frontier. Opportunities for skilled mechanics would multiply who, like him, could romance with these towering titans of sustainability. The winds of change swirled questions around him. However rapid the growth of this industry is, could there be a workforce readiness to match its pace? He couldn't help but think of technology and virtual simulations to accelerate the preparation of novice technicians, helping them experience the thrill and challenges of deciphering this intricate craft.

The setting sun cast a long shadow of the wind turbine. As the day bid farewell, John D'Amico was left in the quiet meditation of his long cherished dream and its underlying complexities–what must we do to ensure a future where wind energy doesn't just boom, but it thrives?

Powering the Future: The Rise of Wind Turbine Technicians

Imagine standing atop a towering wind turbine, the swirling wind and vast open skies stretching out before you. As you gaze down at the world below, you can't help but feel a sense of awe and wonder at the sheer power harnessed by these magnificent machines. What you may not realise, however, is that you could have a pivotal role in ushering in a new era of clean, renewable energy.

In a world where sustainable solutions are becoming increasingly essential, wind energy has emerged as a vital power source. As traditional energy sources dwindle and the effects of climate change become more apparent, the demand for renewable energy has skyrocketed. Harnessing the wind's kinetic energy to generate electricity has proven to be one of the most promising alternatives, making wind turbines an essential component in our quest for a sustainable future.

But who will install and maintain these towering giants? Enter the wind turbine technician: a skilled and essential professional who ensures the smooth operation of these remarkable machines. As wind energy continues to gain traction, job opportunities in this field are soaring. It's an industry poised for exponential growth, creating a path towards a stable and rewarding career without the need for a formal degree.

Wind turbine technicians play a crucial role in the installation, operation, and maintenance of wind turbines. Their responsibilities span from assembling and erecting these impressive structures to performing routine inspections and repairs to optimise performance. They are the unsung heroes who ensure that these towering miracles of engineering keep spinning, efficiently harnessing the power of the wind.

The skills and qualifications needed to become a wind turbine technician are diverse, but not insurmountable. While some formal training in electrical or mechanical systems is beneficial, there are various pathways to enter the field that do not require a traditional four-year degree. Certifications and apprenticeships are becoming increasingly recognized as valid routes to acquire the necessary skills and knowledge.

A career as a wind turbine technician offers stability, growth, and the opportunity to make a meaningful impact on the world. As the demand for wind energy continues to surge, so too will the need for skilled technicians who can keep up with the pace of technological advancements. This chapter will delve into the increasing importance of wind energy, explore the job opportunities in installing and maintaining wind turbines, and provide valuable insights into the skills and qualifications needed to pursue a career in this promising field.

So, if you've ever dreamed of working with your hands, making a tangible difference, and being at the forefront of a sustainable revolution, the world of wind turbine technicians beckons. Join us on this exciting journey as we explore the incredible potential of wind energy and the rewarding career opportunities it presents. Together, we can tap into the power of the wind and usher in a cleaner, more sustainable future for generations to come.

Wind energy is a powerful force that has been harnessed by humans for centuries. In the past, windmills were used for a variety of tasks, from grinding grain to pumping water. But today, wind energy has taken on a whole new importance. As we strive for a more sustainable future, wind power has become an increasingly vital source of clean, renewable energy.

Unlike fossil fuels, which contribute to pollution and climate change, wind energy is clean and unlimited. The power of the wind can be converted into electricity by wind turbines, which consist of large blades that spin in the wind, generating power. These turbines can be found all over the world, in both onshore and offshore locations.

The rise of wind energy can be attributed to a number of factors. First and foremost, it is an abundant and renewable resource. The wind is always blowing somewhere, making it a reliable source of power. In addition, wind energy is cost-effective. Once a wind turbine is installed, the wind itself provides the power at no additional cost. And finally, wind energy is environmentally friendly. It produces no greenhouse gas emissions or air pollution, making it a sustainable alternative to fossil fuels.

As wind energy becomes more important, the demand for skilled professionals to install and maintain wind turbines is growing. This means that there are job opportunities aplenty in the field of wind turbine technology. These technicians play a crucial role in the development of wind energy projects, ensuring that turbines are installed correctly and operating at maximum efficiency.

The job of a wind turbine technician is both challenging and rewarding. Technicians are responsible for installing and maintaining wind turbines, performing routine inspections, and troubleshooting any issues that arise. They must have a strong technical background, with knowledge of electrical systems and mechanical components. In addition, they must be able to work at heights and in various weather conditions.

A career as a wind turbine technician can provide job security and opportunities for growth. As the demand for wind energy continues to rise, the need for skilled technicians will only increase. In fact, the Bureau of Labor Statistics predicts that employment in this field will grow much faster than the average for all occupations.

If you have a passion for renewable energy and a desire to make a positive impact on the environment, a career as a wind turbine technician could be the perfect fit for you. With the right skills and qualifications, you can play a vital role in the development of a more sustainable future. So why wait? Dive into the world of wind energy and explore the possibilities that await you.

By harnessing the power of the wind, we can create a more sustainable future for ourselves and future generations. In the next section, we will delve deeper into the job opportunities that exist in installing and maintaining wind turbines.

When it comes to wind turbine technicians, the demand for their expertise is steadily increasing. As more wind farms are built around the world, the need for skilled individuals to install and maintain these turbines becomes paramount. According to the U.S.

Bureau of Labor Statistics, the employment of wind turbine service technicians is projected to grow by **61 percent** from 2019 to 2029, which is much faster than the average for all occupations. This growth is driven by the expansion of wind energy capacity and the need to maintain existing wind turbines.

So, what does a wind turbine technician do? These technicians are responsible for installing, maintaining, and repairing wind turbines. This can include tasks such as climbing wind turbine towers to perform inspections and repairs, replacing parts, and troubleshooting electrical and mechanical issues. They work on both onshore and offshore wind farms, ensuring that the turbines are operating efficiently and generating electricity.

But it's not just about getting your hands dirty. Wind turbine technicians also work with advanced technology and complex systems. They use specialised tools and equipment to diagnose problems and make repairs. Additionally, they may need to analyse data and perform regular maintenance to prevent potential issues. It's a job that requires a combination of technical skills, physical stamina, and a keen eye for detail.

Now, you might be wondering about the qualifications and skills needed to pursue a career as a wind turbine technician. While a formal degree is not always required, obtaining a postsecondary certificate or an associate's degree in wind energy technology or a related field can greatly enhance your chances of securing a job in this field. These programs typically cover topics such as electrical systems, hydraulic systems, and wind turbine operation and maintenance.

Beyond formal education, there are certain qualities and skills that can help you excel as a wind turbine technician. Problem-solving skills, mechanical aptitude, physical fitness, and the ability to work at heights are all essential in this field. Additionally, strong communication skills and the ability to work well in a team are valuable assets as wind turbine technicians often collaborate with other professionals and contractors.

As we delve deeper into the world of wind turbine technicians, it's important to gain insights into the skills and qualifications needed to pursue a career in this field. While many people may think that becoming a wind turbine technician requires years of schooling and a formal degree, the truth is that there are alternative paths to success in this industry.

In addition to technical skills, there are a few important qualifications for aspiring wind turbine technicians. Firstly, a strong attention to detail is crucial, as even a small error can have significant consequences when working with intricate machinery. Secondly, problem-solving skills are essential, as technicians must be able to quickly and efficiently diagnose and resolve issues. Finally, strong communication and teamwork skills are important, as wind turbine technicians often work in teams and need to be able to effectively communicate with their colleagues.

In conclusion, pursuing a career as a wind turbine technician does not necessarily require a formal degree. While technical skills and qualifications are important, there are alternative paths to success in this industry. Whether through apprenticeship programs, on-the-job training, or continuing education, individuals with the right mix of skills and determination can thrive in this growing field. As the importance of wind energy continues to rise, there will be increasing job opportunities for those who are willing to harness the power of the wind.

Thrive in a Changing Economy

As we come to the end of this chapter, let's take a moment to reflect on what we've learned about the exciting field of wind turbine technicians. We began by exploring the increasing importance of wind energy as a sustainable power source. We delved into the immense potential of harnessing the wind, and how it can play a significant role in reducing our dependence on fossil fuels and combating climate change.

Next, we uncovered the job opportunities in installing and maintaining wind turbines. We discovered that wind turbine technicians are the backbone of the wind energy industry, responsible for keeping these towering structures running smoothly and efficiently. We imagine the thrill of working high above the ground, amidst a sea of blades spinning gracefully in the wind.

But what does it take to pursue a career as a wind turbine technician? We gained insights into the skills and qualifications needed to excel in this field. We learned that a strong foundation in mathematics and mechanical aptitude is essential, along with the ability to troubleshoot and work well in a team. We were inspired by stories of individuals who obtained their skills through on-the-job training and certification programs, proving that you don't always need a formal degree to thrive in a high-demand career.

In closing, we invite you to imagine yourself on top of a wind turbine, feeling the exhilarating rush of the wind against your face. Can you envision the sense of accomplishment that comes from knowing that you're helping to power homes, businesses, and communities with clean, renewable energy? As wind energy becomes more vital, let's remember that the rise of wind turbine technicians is just beginning. So, whether you're starting from scratch or looking to pivot in your career, the path to becoming a wind turbine technician may well be the one that leads you to a sustainable and fulfilling future.

4: Community Gardeners And Urban Farmers

The green economy should not just be about reclaiming throw-away stuff. It should be about reclaiming thrown-away communities. It should not just be about recycling things to give them a second life. We should also be gathering up people and giving them a second chance.

Van Jones

Scarlett, a local from a bustling metropolis, had always found her rhythm much like a busy bee; scampering from her urban dwelling, she flew to corporal cubicles arrayed among towers of glass and steel. The transformation, however, started to unfold one ordinary Sunday afternoon when on a leisurely hike. Suddenly, she noticed an old, dilapidated structure, standing incongruously like a solitary sunflower amid concrete wasteland. It was an abandoned community garden, its skeletal remains still resonating with echoes of once thriving greeneries forgotten in the urban rush.

Visiting this ghost of a garden sparked something inside Scarlett. She shut her eyes and imagined the building in its vibrant past, the spaces teeming with lush tomato vines, perky peppers, and proud sunflowers bathing under the city's filtered sunlight. She could almost get a whiff of sweet fruits waiting to be picked or the earthy aroma of fertile soil yearning for tending hands. The decaying walls seemed to whisper tales of a community that bonded over nurturing nature, finding solace in cohabitation with earth amid a world composed of cold iron and lifeless tar. Scarlett felt an uncanny connection to this deserted testament of life and greenery and started questioning her existence and purpose in the significant design of life.

The idea of cultivating her own harvest, gaining dominion over her nutrients, and being part of a self-reliant community began percolating in her mind. These thoughts started sprouting like a dormant sweet-pea ready to unfurl under the warmth of care and nourishment. Probing into her newfound interest, she faced the fears looming over her, akin to dark clouds over an abandoned field. With the earth bearing the brunt of human exploitation and resources dwindling, wouldn't it make sense to embrace small-scale, community-centric solutions? Perhaps the principles of self-reliance and communal wisdom needed nurturing as much as the crops they yielded?

Returning home, Scarlett's mind clicked back to the skeletal community garden. She perceived the potential of her high-rise balcony - why not foster a few pots of herbs and vegetables there? Perhaps a sturdy tomato plant or a cluster of fragrant basil would be a good start. Tending to these plants, she discovered, began to fill a void within her. Caring for their needs and delighting in their growth journey unpacked an intimate connection with these seedlings, reverberating a 'yes' to life and a new-found faith in the grace of beginnings and ends woven in each seed.

As Scarlett transformed her balcony into a mini oasis and other city-dwellers followed suit, one can't help but raise an intriguing thought - Are we on the verge of a resurgence of urban farming?

The Future of Food: How Community Gardeners and Urban Farmers Will Feed Our Cities

Welcome to Chapter 4 of *Thrive in a Changing Economy: Alternative Careers for a Sustainable Future*. In this chapter, we delve into the world of community gardeners and urban farmers and explore the crucial role they play in cultivating the future of food.

Imagine a bustling city, with towering buildings and busy streets. Now, picture rows of vibrant green plants and bustling bees in the same urban landscape. It may seem like an unlikely pairing, but community gardeners and urban farmers are making it a reality.

1. Understand the need for localised food production and the role of community gardeners and urban farmers in meeting this demand.

As resources become scarce and expensive, the ability to grow food locally, even in urban settings, becomes essential. Community gardeners and urban farmers are at the forefront of this movement, contributing to the production of fresh, nutritious food that is accessible to all.

By cultivating small plots of land in their neighbourhoods or converting unused spaces into fruitful gardens, these individuals are reducing the need for long-distance transportation and the carbon emissions associated with it. They are also increasing food security by bringing fresh produce to areas that may not have easy access to grocery stores or farmers' markets. In the face of a changing climate and an uncertain global economy, the importance of localised food production cannot be overstated.

2. Explore the opportunities for small-scale, intensive agriculture in urban settings.

Urban environments may seem inhospitable to farming, but community gardeners and urban farmers are proving otherwise. Using innovative techniques such as vertical farming, hydroponics, and rooftop gardens, they are transforming urban spaces into thriving agricultural hubs.

These alternative methods of cultivation allow for higher yields in smaller spaces, making urban farming a viable career option. Additionally, the demand for organic and locally-grown produce is on the rise, creating new market opportunities for urban farmers. As the appetite for sustainable and healthy food grows, so do the prospects for those with a knack for urban agriculture.

3. Learn the skills and techniques required to succeed as a community gardener or urban farmer.

Becoming a successful community gardener or urban farmer requires more than just a green thumb. It involves a deep understanding of plant biology, soil health, crop rotation, pest management, and sustainable farming practices. This knowledge can be acquired through formal education, apprenticeships, or hands-on experience.

Equally important is the ability to engage and collaborate with the community. Community gardeners and urban farmers often work closely with residents, local organisations, and policymakers to create sustainable food systems that benefit all. Strong communication and interpersonal skills are essential to foster partnerships and build support for these initiatives.

Cultivating the Future: A Step-by-Step Process

Now that you understand the importance of community gardeners and urban farmers in creating a sustainable future, let's explore a step-by-step process to help you embark on this rewarding career path.

1. **Research the local landscape:** Start by familiarising yourself with the unique characteristics of your area, including climate, soil type, and available resources. This will help you determine the most suitable crops for your urban farm or community garden.
2. **Gain knowledge and skills:** Acquire the necessary knowledge and skills through formal education, workshops, online courses, or mentorship from experienced farmers. Learn about sustainable farming practices, plant biology, pest management, and urban agriculture techniques.
3. **Identify your target market:** Research the demand for locally-grown produce in your area. Are there particular crops that are in high demand? Identify potential customers, such as restaurants, farmers' markets, and community-supported agriculture programs.
4. **Secure land or find alternative growing spaces:** Depending on your available resources, you may choose to lease or purchase land for your farm. If land is scarce or expensive, explore alternative growing spaces such as rooftop gardens, vertical farming systems, or community gardens.
5. **Build a network:** Connect with other community gardeners, urban farmers, and local organisations involved in sustainable agriculture. Attend industry events, workshops, and conferences to expand your knowledge and network.

6. **Engage with the community:** Collaborate with residents, local organisations, and policymakers to create a shared vision for sustainable food systems. Educate and involve the community in your farming initiatives, emphasising the environmental and health benefits of locally-grown food.
7. **Implement sustainable practices:** Prioritise sustainable farming practices, such as composting, water conservation, and organic pest management. Minimise the use of synthetic fertilisers and pesticides, and explore natural alternatives.
8. **Market and sell your produce:** Develop a marketing strategy to sell your produce to potential customers. This could include direct sales at farmers' markets, establishing a community-supported agriculture program, or partnering with local restaurants and grocery stores.
9. **Evaluate and adapt:** Continuously assess the success of your farming endeavours and adapt accordingly. Monitor crop yields, customer feedback, and the impact on the community. Make adjustments to your practices to optimise productivity and sustainability.
10. **Celebrate and share your success:** Share your achievements and inspire others to embrace sustainable agriculture. Host workshops, give talks, or write articles to raise awareness about the importance of community gardeners and urban farmers in feeding our cities.

By following this step-by-step process, you can cultivate a successful career as a community gardener or urban farmer, enriching both your life and the lives of those around you. Together, we can build a future where fresh, nutritious food is accessible to all, and our cities bloom with sustainable agriculture.

When we think of farming, we often envision sprawling fields, tractors, and vast landscapes. But what if I told you that farming could happen right in the heart of a bustling city? That's right – community gardeners and urban farmers are cultivating the future by growing food locally in urban settings. This may seem like a paradox, but it's a growing trend that is poised to play a crucial role in our future food system.

As resources become scarcer and more expensive, the ability to grow food locally becomes essential. It not only reduces our dependence on long-distance transportation but also minimises the environmental impact of food production. By growing food in our own neighbourhoods, we can reduce carbon emissions, conserve water, and preserve biodiversity. But who will take up the mantle of community gardening and urban farming? That's where you come in.

Community gardeners and urban farmers are the unsung heroes of our food system. They are the individuals who transform abandoned lots into thriving vegetable patches and turn empty rooftops into lush gardens. They are the ones who bring fresh, nutritious food to urban communities, where access to healthy options can be limited. But their work goes beyond just growing food. They also educate their communities about sustainable growing practices and inspire others to take up the cause.

Imagine wandering through a bustling cityscape and stumbling upon a hidden oasis of green. The air is filled with the sweet scent of flowers and the earthy aroma of freshly turned soil. The sound of birds chirping and the rustling of leaves provide a welcome respite from the noise of the city. This is the beauty of community gardening and urban farming – it brings nature back into our urban spaces and reconnects us with the land.

But it's not just about the aesthetics. Urban farming has the power to transform communities, both socially and economically. By involving local residents in the process of growing food, community gardens become a space for social interaction, fostering a sense of belonging and empowerment. These gardens can also provide an opportunity for entrepreneurship, as surplus produce can be sold or distributed within the community.

Now, you might be thinking, "I don't have a green thumb," or "I live in a tiny apartment, how can I grow food?" Don't worry – community gardening and urban farming are all about adaptability. Even if you don't have access to a plot of land, you can still get involved by supporting local initiatives or volunteering at community gardens. And who knows, you might discover a passion for growing food that you never knew you had.

So, are you ready to join the ranks of community gardeners and urban farmers? Let's continue our exploration of the opportunities and skills needed to thrive in this exciting field.

Urban settings may not be the first place you think of when it comes to agriculture. Towering skyscrapers and bustling city streets don't exactly conjure images of lush green fields and sprawling farmland. But the truth is, urban areas are becoming important hubs for small-scale, intensive agriculture. Community gardeners and urban farmers are finding innovative ways to grow food right in the heart of the city, and their work is crucial in meeting the demand for localised food production.

In cities, space is at a premium. You won't find vast acres of land waiting to be cultivated. But that hasn't stopped community gardeners and urban farmers from finding creative solutions. They make the most of every available space, transforming rooftops, empty lots, and even small pockets of land into productive growing spaces. Vertical gardens, hydroponics, and rooftop farms are just a few examples of the innovative techniques being used to maximise space and produce food in urban settings.

These urban agriculture projects are about more than just growing food. They're about building communities and fostering connections between people and the food they eat. Community gardeners and urban farmers often organise workshops and events to educate the public about sustainable agriculture and healthy eating. They provide a space for people to come together, learn from one another, and share in the joys of growing their own food. In a world where many of us feel disconnected from the sources of our food, these projects offer a sense of belonging and a way for people to take control of their own food supply. Look for your nearest green spaces and community spaces.

But the benefits of urban agriculture go beyond community building. By growing food locally, we reduce our reliance on long-distance transportation and the carbon emissions associated with it. We also reduce the need for harmful pesticides and fertilisers, and lessen the strain on our already stretched resources. In a world facing uncertain climate change and growing populations, the ability to grow food locally, even in urban settings, is essential. Community gardeners and urban farmers are at the forefront of this movement, showing us that it is possible to live sustainably in the city.

So how can you get involved in urban agriculture? The first step is to learn as much as you can about sustainable agriculture practices. Understanding the principles of organic gardening, permaculture, and hydroponics will be invaluable as you begin your journey. Look for local workshops, courses, and online resources that can help you gain the knowledge and skills you need. Once you feel confident in your abilities, seek out opportunities to get hands-on experience. Join a community garden, volunteer at an urban farm, or even start your own small-scale project. The more you practise, the more you'll learn, and the better equipped you'll be to make a difference in your own community.

Urban agriculture is more than just a trend. It's a vital part of our future if we want to build a sustainable food system. So why not take a leap of faith and get involved? Whether you're a seasoned gardener or a complete beginner, there's a place for you in the world of community gardening and urban farming. Join the movement and be a part of something bigger than yourself. Together, we can cultivate a future where everyone has access to healthy, locally grown food.

Building a Strong Foundation: The Framework for Community Gardening and Urban Farming

Now that we understand the need for localised food production and the opportunities that lie in community gardening and urban farming, let's delve into the skills and techniques required for success in these fields. Picture this section as the framework, the blueprint that will guide you as you embark on your journey towards becoming a community gardener or urban farmer.

The Framework: Cultivating Success

In this section, we will introduce a model that encapsulates the key components and interrelationships involved in community gardening and urban farming. This framework will serve as a guide, providing clarity and a roadmap as you navigate the world of sustainable agriculture. So, let's dive into the garden and explore each component of this model, unravelling the secrets to success in this field.

Component 1: Knowledge and Expertise

The first pillar of our framework is knowledge and expertise. Just like a sturdy foundation, this component forms the basis for everything that follows. Acquiring knowledge about sustainable agriculture, crop rotation, soil health, and pest management is essential for long-term success. You can seek this knowledge through formal education, online courses, workshops, or by learning from experienced mentors in the field. By continually expanding your expertise, you will become a valuable resource in your community and contribute to the growth of sustainable practices.

Component 2: Resource Management

Resource management is the second component in our framework. Like a gardener tending to their plot, you must be adept at managing the resources available to you. This includes not only the physical resources such as land, water, and tools but also the human and financial resources. Efficiently allocating and utilising these resources will enable you to maximise productivity and minimise waste. By implementing sustainable practices, you will contribute to the resilience of your community and protect the environment for future generations.

Component 3: Community Engagement

Community engagement is the lifeblood of community gardening and urban farming. Just as the plants in a garden thrive when nurtured by a caring gardener, these practices flourish when supported by an engaged and passionate community. Building relationships, collaborating with local organisations, and educating the community about the benefits of sustainable agriculture are crucial in creating a resilient and connected food system. By fostering a sense of ownership and collective responsibility, you will empower your community to take charge of their food security and well-being.

Component 4: Adaptability and Innovation

In an ever-changing world, adaptability and innovation are essential qualities for community gardeners and urban farmers. Just as a skilled gardener adjusts their cultivation practices to account for changing weather conditions, you must be able to adapt to new challenges and find innovative solutions. By experimenting with new methods, technologies, and plant varieties, you can enhance productivity and overcome obstacles. Embracing a growth mindset and continuously seeking improved practices will set you apart as a resilient and forward-thinking practitioner.

Component 5: Environmental Stewardship

The final component in our framework is environmental stewardship. In a time when our planet is facing numerous challenges, it is crucial that community gardeners and urban farmers prioritise sustainable and regenerative practices. By nurturing the soil, conserving water, and using organic fertilisers, you can create a thriving ecosystem that supports biodiversity and mitigates climate change. By being mindful of your environmental impact, you will not only nourish your community but also contribute to the well-being of the planet as a whole.

Thrive in a Changing Economy

At the heart of local environmental stewardship is the recognition that everyone has a part to play in maintaining the health and vitality of the environment that surrounds them. This can take various forms, from small, everyday actions to larger community-led initiatives. Simple acts like reducing waste, recycling, using environmentally friendly products, and conserving water and energy contribute significantly to local environmental health. These practices, when adopted widely, can lead to substantial positive impacts on air and water quality, wildlife habitats, and overall ecosystem health.

Effective stewardship often involves partnerships between local residents, businesses, non-profits, and government agencies. These collaborations can lead to more comprehensive and effective approaches to managing local environmental issues, such as pollution, habitat destruction, and climate change adaptation.

As you can see, each component of our framework is interconnected, forming a delicate web of knowledge, resource management, community engagement, adaptability, and environmental stewardship. By embracing these principles and building upon them, you will cultivate not only a fulfilling career but also a bright and sustainable future for yourself and your community.

Now that we have explored the framework, let's dive deeper into each component, exploring the intricacies and practical applications that will empower you to thrive as a community gardener or urban farmer. Grab your gardening gloves and let's get started!

Community gardeners and urban farmers. They may not have the traditional education credentials that society often values, but their skills and contributions are indispensable in our changing world. They understand the need for localised food production and the vital role they play in meeting this demand. In this chapter, we've explored the opportunities that exist for small-scale, intensive agriculture in urban settings, and we've learned about the skills and techniques required to excel in this field. As we conclude this chapter, it's important to reflect on the profound impact that community gardeners and urban farmers can have on our future.

Picture this: row after row of vibrant green vegetables, blooming flowers, and the hum of bees drifting through the air. There's a sense of calm and purpose in a community garden or an urban farm. These small patches of land, nestled in the heart of our cities, are a testament to the ingenuity and resilience of those who tend them. They are a living example of how we can reclaim our connection to the earth and nourish ourselves in a sustainable way.

But why is localised food production so important? In a world where resources are becoming scarcer and more expensive, the ability to produce food locally is not just a luxury, it's a necessity. When we rely on large-scale industrial agriculture, we are at the mercy of fluctuating markets, climate change, and the long supply chains that transport our food from faraway places. By growing food close to where it's consumed, we reduce our dependence on these external factors and gain control over our own sustenance.

Community gardeners and urban farmers are at the forefront of this movement towards localised food production. They have taken it upon themselves to transform neglected plots of land into thriving oases of greenery. They have turned rooftops, balconies, and empty lots into productive spaces where fresh fruits and vegetables can flourish. Their work not only provides nourishment for their communities, but it also brings people together, fosters a sense of ownership and pride, and reconnects us with the natural world.

To succeed as a community gardener or urban farmer, one must possess a unique set of skills and knowledge. From understanding soil health and plant biology to managing pests and maximising space, these individuals are the true masters of their craft. They know how to make the most of limited resources, utilising composting, rainwater harvesting, and other sustainable practices to minimise waste and conserve water. They are problem solvers, constantly adapting to the challenges presented by urban environments, and finding innovative solutions to grow food in unconventional spaces.

But it's not just about the technical skills. Community gardeners and urban farmers also possess an innate sense of stewardship and a deep connection to the land. They recognize that the earth is a living organism, and they treat it with the respect it deserves. They revel in the joy of nurturing a tiny seedling into a bountiful harvest, and they understand the profound impact that this simple act can have on their communities and the planet as a whole.

So, as we look to the future, let us remember the importance of localised food production and the crucial role that community gardeners and urban farmers play in creating a sustainable and resilient food system. They are the unsung heroes of our cities, quietly tending to their gardens and farms, and making a real difference in the lives of those around them. Their work is a reminder that a better, more sustainable world is possible, and that each one of us has the power to cultivate it. Whether you have ample land or just a windowsill, there is a place for you in this movement. So go ahead, get your hands dirty, and join the growing community of gardeners and farmers who are cultivating a better future for us all. And a challenge- how can we get people to be more interested in this area?

5: Resplendent Recycling Centre Operators

We can't just consume our way to a more sustainable world. - Jennifer Nini

Tom Jenkins, the man with a look of a weathered mariner, had a peculiar bond with discarded things. Old soda cans that once fizzed with life and discarded newspapers with stories untold spoke to him. Even broken glass, shimmering under the sunlight took a beautiful form in his eyes. They weren't just waste dumped uncaringly in the bins and gutters of his small seaside town but treasures often overlooked. Today, ensconced as a manager at the local recycling centre, he felt his enthralling journey finding treasures within the trash heaps had taken on a worldwide significance, in the heart of the resource scarcity conundrum and the hopeful quest for sustainability.

At daybreak, the recycling yard sprung to life under the yawning sun. The cacophonic hum of sorting machines spun an unusual melody mixing with the rustling canvas of aluminium and paper. Amidst this industrial lullaby, he could hear the jittery music of rookies, their excitement barely masking their nervousness, as they learned the ropes. It was a soothing murmur against the relentless machinery and it reassured Tom - life was rolling on here, amid the mountains of detritus in an ever-shifting world.

Under the sweltering gaze of the noon sun, he watched workers threading through debris to maintain their intricate ballet of recycling. At that moment, his concerns escalated. How essential was their work! With mankind's unchecked consumption patterns necessitating recycling operations, separating plastic from paper felt as dire as disarming an explosive device. In an age frantically guzzling resources, weren't these workers standing like sentinels guiding us to a sustainable future? He firmly believed their largely unnoticed endeavours were a quiet shield against any upcoming disaster.

When the sky wore its nighttime cloak speckled with stars, and the workers vanished under the neon radiance of the 'Recycling: The Key to Conservation' sign at the gate, Tom's reflections took a deeper turn. He realised that his earlier dreams of the undisturbed comfort of a white-collar job fell short before the gratifying reality of his current role in resource conservation. Wasn't there nobility in mitigating waste, reclaiming whatever could be given a new life, rather than endlessly running in the corporate rat race? Maybe he was meant to tread on this path after all.

The whispering breeze, dancing merrily through the serene yard and lifting forgotten fragments of the day's work, drew Tom's attention. Seeing nature and human detritus juxtaposed lead him into pondering about his journey and mission. The troubling sight of depleting natural resources, expanding landfills, and escalating consumption patterns could have worn him down. Yet, the thought that his contribution was part of the solution enlivened him. It underlined the worth of his day-to-day battles with waste and reinforced his belief in the power of recycling as a formidable tool for navigating the demanding passage towards sustainability. Wouldn't it be through persevering in such humble roles that humanity could counterbalance its voracious appetite for consumption?

The Silent Heroes: Recycling Centre Operators

In a world where resources are becoming increasingly scarce, the importance of recycling cannot be underestimated. Recycling centre operators are the unsung heroes in the battle against waste and resource depletion. These individuals play a vital role in sorting, processing, and managing recycled materials, ensuring that valuable resources are not lost to landfill but instead given a second life.

Recycling has long been touted as a solution to the growing problem of waste disposal. However, its significance goes far beyond simply reducing the amount of trash we produce. At its core, recycling is about resource management and sustainability. By collecting and repurposing materials that would otherwise end up in landfills, recycling centre operators help to conserve precious resources like metals, paper, and plastic. They enable these materials to be transformed into new products, reducing the need for extracting and manufacturing virgin materials.

The impact of recycling centre operators is far-reaching. Consider the environmental benefits alone. Every ton of paper that is recycled saves 17 trees, 7,000 gallons of water, and enough energy to power the average home for six months. By diverting materials from landfill, these operators are not only conserving resources but also reducing greenhouse gas emissions and preventing pollution caused by the extraction and production of new materials.

But recycling centre operators do more than simply collect and process recyclables. They play a crucial role in educating the public and promoting sustainable habits. They work directly with individuals and businesses, helping them understand the importance of recycling and providing guidance on what can and cannot be recycled. By fostering a culture of sustainability, recycling centre operators contribute to broader systemic change that reduces waste generation and promotes a circular economy.

There are a variety of job roles within the field of recycling centre operations, each with its own unique set of responsibilities. Sorting operatives ensure that materials are properly segregated, removing contaminants and preparing them for processing. Processors use specialised equipment to transform materials into raw commodities that can be used to manufacture new products. Managers oversee the entire operation, ensuring smooth workflow, coordinating logistics, and implementing quality control measures. These diverse roles offer opportunities for individuals with a range of skills and interests to contribute to a more sustainable future.

So, what does it take to be a successful recycling centre operator? While no formal degree is required, a strong foundation in environmental science or sustainability studies can be beneficial. Additionally, practical skills such as problem-solving, attention to detail, and the ability to work in a fast-paced environment are highly valued. Communication skills are also crucial, as recycling centre operators often interact with a wide range of stakeholders, from customers to waste haulers to manufacturers.

Investing in a career in recycling centre operations is not only a sound economic choice but also a way to make a positive impact on the planet. By choosing this path, you become part of the solution, helping to conserve resources, reduce waste, and fight climate change. The demand for recycling centre operators is only going to increase as resources become scarcer and sustainability becomes paramount. So why not consider becoming one of the silent heroes of the recycling industry? Step into the world of recycling centre operations and join the movement towards a more sustainable future.

Recycling is often seen as a mundane task, a chore we do to keep the planet clean. But what if I told you that recycling holds the key to our sustainable future? As physical resources become scarcer, recycling becomes even more critical. This means that jobs in sorting, processing, and managing recycled materials will grow, making recycling centre operators crucial for resource management. Let's explore the significance of recycling in resource management and sustainability, and discover the opportunities it presents for employment.

Our planet's resources are limited, and we must find ways to use them more efficiently. Recycling allows us to give new life to materials that would otherwise end up in landfills or incinerators. By transforming waste into valuable resources, we can reduce the demand for raw materials and decrease energy consumption. Recycling is a key component of the circular economy, where products and materials are reused or repurposed, minimising waste and maximising resource efficiency.

Imagine you're walking through a lush forest, surrounded by towering trees, vibrant flowers, and the gentle chirping of birds. This forest represents our planet, rich in resources and teeming with life. Now, picture a clearing in that forest, filled with piles of discarded materials - plastics, metals, and paper. These materials are not biodegradable, which means they will stay in that clearing indefinitely, slowly suffocating the life around them.

But what if we could take those materials and turn them into something useful again? Imagine a recycling centre as a beacon of hope, a place where those discarded materials can find new purpose. Recycling centre operators are the guardians of this transformation. They ensure that every item that enters the centre is carefully sorted and processed, ready to be transformed into something new.

Recycling centre operators are the unsung heroes of sustainability. They play a crucial role in managing our resources efficiently and reducing our impact on the environment. By separating materials, removing contaminants, and preparing them for the next stage of the recycling process, they ensure that every item is given a second chance. Their work is not glamorous, but it is essential for creating a sustainable future.

But it's not just about making the world a better place. Recycling centre operators are in high demand, and as the importance of recycling grows, so do the opportunities for employment. In addition to sorting and processing materials, there are also roles in logistics, quality control, and facility management. These jobs provide stability, competitive salaries, and room for growth.

So, whether you're passionate about sustainability, want to make a difference in your community, or are simply looking for a secure career, working in a recycling centre could be the perfect fit. With the right skills and knowledge, you can be at the forefront of the recycling revolution, shaping a sustainable future for generations to come.

Are you ready to join the ranks of the recycling centre operators and become a steward of our resources? Let's dive deeper into the various job roles in sorting, processing, and managing recycled materials.

Imagine walking into a recycling centre and being greeted by the bustling sound of machinery sorting and processing materials. The first job role that comes to mind is that of a sorter. Sorters are responsible for separating different types of recyclable materials, such as paper, plastic, glass, and metal. They use their keen eye and attention to detail to ensure that the materials are properly sorted and free from contaminants.

Once the materials have been sorted, they move on to the next stage of the process: processing. Processors are skilled individuals who operate machinery and equipment to transform raw materials into usable products. They may shred paper, melt down plastic, crush glass, or smelt metal, depending on the specific material being processed. This requires technical knowledge and expertise to ensure that the materials are handled safely and efficiently.

Managing recycled materials is another crucial aspect of the job. This role involves overseeing the storage, transportation, and distribution of recycled materials. Managers in recycling centres are responsible for coordinating with various stakeholders, such as manufacturers, wholesalers, and retailers, to ensure a smooth flow of materials. They also monitor market trends and demand to make informed decisions about pricing and distribution.

Working in a recycling centre can be physically demanding as it often involves lifting heavy objects and working in noisy environments. However, it is also highly rewarding. Recycling centre operators have the satisfaction of knowing that they are contributing to resource conservation and environmental sustainability. They are part of a broader movement towards creating a circular economy, where materials are continuously recycled and reused instead of being disposed of as waste.

Acquiring the skills and knowledge needed to work in a recycling centre requires a combination of practical experience and a solid foundation of understanding in waste management and environmental sustainability. While a formal degree may not be necessary, it is important to be well-versed in the processes and principles involved in recycling. In this section, we will explore some key areas of expertise that are helpful for those interested in working in a recycling centre.

First and foremost, a strong understanding of waste management practices is essential. This includes knowledge of different types of waste, their composition, and how they can be recycled or disposed of responsibly. Familiarity with local regulations and guidelines for waste management is also crucial. This knowledge will enable you to ensure that recycling processes are carried out in compliance with legal and environmental requirements.

Apart from these technical skills, communication and teamwork skills are also valuable in a recycling centre. Working in a recycling centre often involves collaboration with colleagues, as well as interaction with customers and external stakeholders. Good communication skills, both verbal and written, are essential for effective collaboration and customer service. Additionally, the ability to work well in a team, adapt to changing circumstances, and solve problems collaboratively is highly valued in this field.

Furthermore, a commitment to environmental sustainability and a passion for making a positive impact on the environment are important qualities for those working in recycling centres. In a world where resources are becoming increasingly hard to find, the role of recycling centre operators in conserving and reusing valuable materials is essential. Being motivated by a sense of purpose and a desire to contribute to a sustainable future can greatly enhance job satisfaction in this field.

A Country Tale

In the quaint town of Bumblebee Corner, where the sun always seemed to shine a tad brighter, Mrs. Agatha Twiddleton made an astonishing discovery that turned her world delightfully topsy-turvy.

Every Thursday, Agatha, with her cat Sir Whiskers in tow, would dutifully wheel her blue recycling bin to the curb. However, one peculiar Thursday, as she lifted the lid of the bin, she was greeted not by the usual suspects of newspapers and empty milk jugs but by a rather confused-looking garden gnome.

The gnome, no taller than a baguette and sporting a hat as red as a fire truck, blinked at her with beady eyes. "Good day," he said, in a voice that sounded like a door squeak.

Agatha, whose life's excitement usually peaked at finding a two-for-one coupon in the mail, nearly dropped her tea mug. "Goodness gracious!" she exclaimed. "How on earth did you end up in my recycling?"

The gnome, whose name tag read 'Gnorman', shrugged his tiny shoulders. "I'm not entirely sure, Mrs. Twiddleton. I remember admiring the moon's luminosity last night and then... poof! Here I am!"

"Well, we can't have you recycled, now can we?" Agatha mused, as Sir Whiskers sniffed suspiciously at Gnorman.

Thrive in a Changing Economy

With a newfound sense of purpose, Agatha and her miniature guest embarked on a mission to unravel the mystery of Gnorman's unexpected journey. Their first stop was Mr. Higgins, the nocturnal baker, known for his love of gnomes and midnight gardening.

"Ah, Gnorman!" exclaimed Mr. Higgins, dusting flour off his apron. "Wandered off again, have we?"

Through a series of chuckles and chortles, Mr. Higgins explained that Gnorman was part of his 'Traveling Gnome Experiment.' He'd been placing gnomes around town to see where they'd end up, courtesy of curious passersby.

Agatha couldn't help but laugh. "Only in Bumblebee Corner," she said, shaking her head.

From that day on, Gnorman the gnome stood proudly in Agatha's garden, regaling her flowers with tales of his brief stint in the recycling bin. Agatha, for her part, made sure to check her bin every Thursday, half-expecting to find a mermaid or perhaps a talking frog.

And as for Sir Whiskers? He never did trust garden gnomes again, especially those with squeaky voices.

Working in a recycling centre offers a unique opportunity to be a part of a growing industry that plays a crucial role in resource management and sustainability. By acquiring the necessary skills and knowledge, you can contribute to the efficient processing of recycled materials, help reduce waste, and make a positive impact on the environment. So, if you are passionate about recycling and eager to create a sustainable future, consider a career in a recycling centre and become a vital player in the journey towards a more sustainable world.

Now, as we conclude this chapter, let's reflect on the "big idea" behind it: the importance of recycling centre operators as resources become scarce. The world we live in is changing rapidly, and it is crucial that we adapt our practices to ensure a sustainable future. One avenue where this adaptation is happening is through recycling.

Think about it for a moment. Every soda can tossed in the trash, every old newspaper left to decay, and every plastic bottle abandoned in a landfill represents a missed opportunity to conserve resources. Instead of being discarded, these items could be recycled, repurposed, and reintroduced into the production cycle. Recycling centre operators hold the key to unlocking this potential and transforming waste into valuable resources.

By embracing a career as a recycling centre operator, you are not only making a positive impact on the environment but also seizing an opportunity for personal and professional growth. As the demand for recycling continues to rise, so does the need for skilled individuals who can efficiently sort, process, and manage recycled materials. This demand opens doors to a wide range of career opportunities, from waste management supervisors to recycling facility managers.

Now, armed with this knowledge and awareness, it's time to take action. Whether you're pursuing a career in recycling or considering expanding your existing skills in the field, remember that every step you take matters. Each plastic bottle you recycle and each paper product you separate from the waste stream contributes to a more sustainable future.

So, let's embrace the transformation from waste to resource and become the change-makers our world needs. Let's recognize the vital role of recycling centre operators in managing our resources and protecting our planet. And let's use our collective power to create a future where sustainability is not just a buzzword but a way of life.

The journey towards a sustainable future starts with you. Let's thrive together in this changing economy, and let recycling be our guiding light on this path of progress.

Keep the momentum going, stay inspired, and never underestimate the impact you can make as a recycling centre operator.

6: Vital Water Harvesting Technicians

No water, no life. No blue, no green.

Sylvia Earle

In the sun-bleached and thirsty desert town, Caleb watched as the cracked and barren earth yearned for moisture. As a water harvesting technician and a keen environmentalist, he longed for the sweet times of his youth when rain nourished the parched ground, enabling a humble farming life. Those were bountiful days of resiliency, of life brimming with hope - a powerful contrast to today's trying times.

From his sun-drenched office, Caleb observed the town's children at play in the dust-blanketed square, their laughter rippling through the tranquil afternoon. Each burst of youthful joy punctuated the harsh reality his precious town faced. These children, so full of promise, played innocently with nature's shortage.

Fueled by resolve, Caleb immersed himself in the plans for his latest endeavour: a cutting-edge rainwater harvesting apparatus. Every tap of his pencil on the weathered desk reflected his inner turmoil; a constant push-pull between despair and optimism, between the funnelling costs of the project and the mammoth impact it would have on his community. Amidst this demanding terrain, Caleb saw himself as a producer of rain – a guardian of survival.

His focus was broken by the rusty ring of the dilapidated brass bell above his door. Standing in the threshold was Aiden, a young man with eyes filled with purpose and a heart consumed by dreams. Caleb knew him as one of the few who resonated with his vision for a sustainable future. Eager to learn and contribute, Aiden represented a flicker of hope in their struggling lands.

The better half of their afternoon teemed with earnest conversation, driven by necessity and duty towards their community. Their discourse consisted of rainwater harvesting methods, intricate details of greywater systems, and the undeniable importance of their craft - life saviours in an unbearable realm. With every exchange, they were fighting not just a crisis; they were sketching the destiny of their town.

As the fervour of daylight succumbed to the flamboyant tints of a desert sunset, specks of dust hanging in the air shivered under the fading radiance. Their mission was far from complete, yet a fresh sense of hope circulated in their town, embodied in these two men determined to reshape their arid fate.

Could they triumph against nature's test and lead the march towards water conservation and sustainability?

The Unsung Heroes of Water Conservation: Water Harvesting Technicians

The world is changing, and with it comes a growing concern for the scarcity of our most precious resource - water. From California's prolonged drought to the water crises in cities like Cape Town and Chennai, the need for water conservation is becoming increasingly urgent. And this is where **water harvesting technicians** come into the picture.

In regions facing water scarcity, the setup and maintenance of rainwater harvesting or greywater systems can be a game-changer. Technologies that capture and reuse rainwater or wastewater from bathrooms and kitchens are not new, but they are gaining widespread recognition for their potential in addressing the water crisis. Water harvesting technicians are the unsung heroes who bring these systems to life and help preserve every precious drop.

Imagine a world where rainwater that would have otherwise gone down the drain is collected and stored for later use. Picture a system that treats and purifies greywater, making it suitable for irrigation or even flushing toilets. These are just a few examples of the innovative solutions that water harvesting technicians make a reality.

Water conservation is at the heart of their work. These technicians understand that in regions facing water scarcity, every drop counts. Through their expertise, they ensure that not a single drop is wasted. They are well-versed in the process of setting up rainwater harvesting and greywater systems, understanding the intricacies of water collection, filtration, and reuse.

To become a water harvesting technician, one needs a diverse set of skills. This profession requires a deep understanding of water management and conservation practices, as well as knowledge of plumbing, filtration systems, and sustainable construction techniques. Water harvesting technicians must also possess problem-solving skills, as they often encounter unique challenges in each installation. They need to be adaptable, flexible, and ready to innovate to find solutions that fit specific environments and requirements.

But it's not just technical skills that make a water harvesting technician successful. They also need to be good communicators, working closely with clients to educate them about the benefits of water conservation and the proper use and maintenance of their systems. Additionally, they must stay updated on the latest advancements and regulations in the field, ensuring that their work meets industry standards.

The ripple effects of water harvesting technicians' work extend far beyond individual installations. By helping communities and businesses reduce their reliance on traditional water sources, they contribute to overall water security. This is especially crucial in areas facing water scarcity, where every drop saved can make a significant difference.

In this chapter, we will delve deeper into the world of water harvesting technicians. We will explore the importance of water conservation and the role these professionals play in addressing water scarcity. We will also take a closer look at the process of setting up and maintaining rainwater harvesting and greywater systems. By understanding the skills and expertise required to pursue a career as a water harvesting technician, we can truly appreciate the importance of their role in building a sustainable future.

So, join me on this journey as we discover the world of water harvesting technicians - the guardians of our most precious resource - who are making a difference, one drop at a time.

Thrive in a Changing Economy

Water scarcity is a pressing issue in many regions around the world. As climate change continues to intensify, water resources are becoming increasingly scarce and valuable. In these areas, every drop of water counts, and it is crucial to find ways to conserve and efficiently use this limited resource.

One of the key strategies for water conservation is rainwater harvesting. This involves collecting and storing rainwater for later use. By capturing rainwater, we can reduce our reliance on other sources of water, such as groundwater or surface water. Rainwater harvesting systems can be as simple as collecting water in buckets or more complex, involving the installation of underground storage tanks and filtration systems.

Another important approach to water conservation is the use of greywater systems. Greywater is wastewater generated from activities such as showering, laundry, and dishwashing. Instead of letting this water go to waste, greywater systems collect and treat it for reuse, typically for purposes like toilet flushing, garden irrigation, or even purifying it for household use.

By implementing rainwater harvesting and greywater systems, we can ensure that every drop of water is put to good use. These systems not only help conserve water but also reduce the strain on existing water sources. In regions facing water scarcity, they can be a lifeline, providing a reliable and sustainable water supply.

But setting up and maintaining these systems requires specialised knowledge and expertise. This is where water harvesting technicians come in. These professionals have the skills to design, install, and maintain rainwater harvesting and greywater systems. They understand the complexities of water management and can help ensure the efficient and effective use of water resources.

Thrive in a Changing Economy

Water harvesting technicians play a vital role in water conservation efforts. They can help homeowners, businesses, and communities make the most of their available water resources. Whether it's designing a rainwater harvesting system for a residential property or helping a commercial establishment implement a greywater system, these technicians have the know-how to make it happen.

The demand for water harvesting technicians is likely to increase in the coming years as water scarcity becomes a more prominent issue. As more people recognize the importance of water conservation and the value of sustainable water management practices, the need for skilled technicians will grow. This presents an excellent opportunity for those interested in pursuing a career in water management.

Water harvesting technicians have the chance to make a real difference in the world. By helping communities utilise their water resources more effectively, they contribute to the preservation of this vital and limited resource. They are the custodians of water, safeguarding it for future generations.

Are you intrigued by the idea of becoming a water harvesting technician? Let's dive deeper into the process of setting up and maintaining rainwater harvesting and greywater systems.

Understanding the process of setting up and maintaining rainwater harvesting and greywater systems is crucial for addressing water scarcity in regions facing this challenge. These systems play a vital role in preserving water and ensuring sustainable use. By capturing rainwater and reusing greywater, individuals and communities can make a significant impact in conserving water resources.

Setting up rainwater harvesting systems

Rainwater harvesting systems are designed to collect and store rainwater for various uses. The setup process involves a few key steps. First, a suitable location for installing the system needs to be identified. This could be a rooftop, a paved surface, or even a garden. The area should be able to capture a significant amount of rainwater during rainfall events.

Next, a collection system needs to be implemented. This typically involves installing gutters and downspouts to direct rainwater from the roof or surface into a storage tank or reservoir. Proper filtration mechanisms should be in place to remove debris and prevent the entry of contaminants into the storage system.

Maintaining rainwater harvesting systems

Once the rainwater harvesting system is set up, regular maintenance is essential to ensure its effective functioning. This includes periodic inspection and cleaning of gutters, downspouts, and filters to prevent blockages. The storage tank should also be checked for any signs of damage or leaks.

Proper water management is crucial to prevent stagnation and the growth of bacteria or algae in the storage tank. Regularly using the stored rainwater for irrigation, cleaning, or toilet flushing helps maintain the water's freshness and prevents any buildup of impurities.

Setting up greywater systems

Greywater refers to wastewater generated from domestic activities such as showering, washing dishes, or doing laundry. Capturing and treating greywater can significantly reduce water usage in households. Setting up a greywater system involves a few key steps.

First, the greywater needs to be collected and treated. This can be done by diverting the greywater from the source, such as a shower or sink, to a treatment system. The treatment process may involve filtration, disinfection, or the use of specific technologies to remove impurities and make the water safe for reuse.

Maintaining greywater systems

Regular maintenance is crucial to ensure the efficient functioning of greywater systems. This includes cleaning and inspecting pipes, filters, and treatment systems to prevent blockages and ensure the quality of the treated greywater.

It is also important to follow appropriate guidelines when using greywater for different purposes. For example, greywater used for irrigation should be applied to the soil rather than direct contact with edible plants. Adhering to these guidelines helps ensure the health and safety of individuals and the environment.

Understanding the process of setting up and maintaining rainwater harvesting and greywater systems is vital for addressing water scarcity. By implementing these systems and practising responsible water management, individuals and communities can make a significant impact in conserving water resources and promoting sustainability. Water harvesting technicians play a crucial role in ensuring the efficient and effective operation of these systems, further highlighting the importance of their expertise in water management.

Explore the skills and expertise required to pursue a career as a water harvesting technician.

Welcome back! Now that we understand the importance of water conservation in regions facing water scarcity, and we've delved into the process of setting up and maintaining rainwater harvesting and greywater systems, let's explore the skills and expertise required to pursue a career as a water harvesting technician.

Becoming a water harvesting technician requires a unique set of skills and knowledge. It's not just about understanding the technical aspects of rainwater harvesting and greywater systems; it's also about being able to assess water availability, analyse water quality, and design efficient water management plans.

A water harvesting technician needs a solid foundation in the principles of hydrology and water management. By understanding how water moves through a landscape, they can identify potential sources of water and develop strategies for capturing and utilising it effectively. This knowledge allows them to evaluate the feasibility and sustainability of different water harvesting projects.

In addition to hydrology, a water harvesting technician should also have a good understanding of plumbing and water distribution systems. This knowledge is essential for designing and implementing rainwater harvesting and greywater systems. They need to know how to install tanks, pipes, and pumps, and how to ensure proper flow and distribution of water.

Furthermore, a water harvesting technician should possess strong problem-solving and critical thinking skills. They will face unique challenges in each project they undertake, and they need to be able to analyse these challenges and come up with creative solutions. Whether it's overcoming design limitations, optimising water storage, or addressing water quality issues, their ability to think outside the box will be crucial.

Communication and interpersonal skills are also essential for a water harvesting technician. They will be working closely with clients, other technicians, and potentially even government officials. Being able to effectively communicate the benefits of water harvesting and address any concerns or questions will be crucial for their success. Additionally, they may need to collaborate with other professionals, such as engineers or environmental scientists, so being able to work well in a team setting is important.

Finally, a water harvesting technician should have a strong commitment to sustainability and a passion for environmental conservation. They are on the front lines of efforts to reduce water waste and promote more efficient water use. Their work directly contributes to the preservation of our precious water resources, so a deep appreciation for the environment and a desire to make a positive impact are essential qualities.

In conclusion, a career as a water harvesting technician is not only fulfilling, but it also plays a vital role in ensuring the sustainable use of water in regions facing scarcity. By honing their skills in hydrology, plumbing, problem-solving, and communication, these technicians have the opportunity to make a real difference. They are the experts who will design and maintain the systems that will enable communities to preserve every drop of water.

Thrive in a Changing Economy

Our Future Depends on Water Harvesting Technicians

As we reach the end of this chapter, it's clear that the role of water harvesting technicians will be crucial in our ever-changing world. Water scarcity is becoming a pressing issue in many regions, making it essential for us to recognize the importance of water conservation. By setting up and maintaining rainwater harvesting and greywater systems, we can ensure the efficient and sustainable use of every precious drop.

Imagine a world where water scarcity is no longer a threatening reality. A world where communities can thrive and flourish, confident in their water supply. Now, imagine being part of the solution, playing a pivotal role in making this vision a reality. That's exactly what a water harvesting technician does.

By understanding the process of water conservation, you'll have the power to transform landscapes and preserve one of our most vital resources. Whether it's capturing rainwater from rooftops or diverting and treating greywater, your skills will be instrumental in preserving every precious drop. And trust me, **it's a skillset that will be in high demand**.

But what does it take to become a water harvesting technician? It's not as daunting as it may seem. Sure, it requires knowledge, expertise, and a willingness to learn, but with the right training and experience, you can excel in this field. As a technician, you will be responsible for installing rainwater harvesting systems, creating and maintaining storage tanks, and ensuring optimum water quality for indoor and outdoor uses. Your work will contribute to a more sustainable future and positively impact the lives of countless individuals and communities.

The Skills and Expertise Required

To pursue a career as a water harvesting technician, there are a few essential skills and expertise you'll need to develop. First and foremost, you'll need a solid understanding of water systems, both traditional and alternative. This knowledge will enable you to assess the needs of a specific area and design tailored solutions that maximise water capture and reuse.

Additionally, proficiency in plumbing, construction, and landscaping will be invaluable. As a water harvesting technician, you'll be involved in the installation and maintenance of various components, such as gutters, pipelines, filtration systems, and storage tanks. It's essential to have a good grasp of these disciplines to ensure the efficiency and longevity of the systems you work on.

Attention to detail is another crucial skill for a water harvesting technician. The success of a water harvesting system relies on careful planning and meticulous execution. From assessing the location and slope of a property to calculating the optimal storage capacity, every decision you make will impact the efficiency of the system. Being thorough and methodical will contribute to the long-term success of your projects.

- Finally, as a water harvesting technician, **you must stay up to date with the latest advancements in technology and techniques**. Innovations in sustainable water management are constantly evolving, and it's vital to stay informed. Attending workshops, conferences, and continuing education courses will enhance your knowledge and keep your skills sharp.

Lookout for new advances like:
- Fog Harvesting: This innovative technique involves collecting water from fog using large mesh nets. The fog passes through the nets, condenses into water droplets, and is then collected in reservoirs. Recent advancements have improved the efficiency of these nets, making them a viable water source in fog-prone, arid regions.
- Smart Rainwater Harvesting Systems: The integration of smart technology into rainwater harvesting has significantly improved its efficiency and usability. These systems use sensors and automated controls to optimize the collection and storage of rainwater, ensure water quality, and reduce maintenance. They can be programmed to respond to weather forecasts and water demand.
- Atmospheric Water Generators (AWG): AWGs extract water from humid ambient air. Recent advancements have increased their efficiency, making them a practical solution in humid environments. These systems use refrigeration techniques to condense moisture from the air and collect it as water, even in areas where surface and groundwater are scarce.
- Permeable Pavements and Green Roofs: These urban water harvesting solutions help manage stormwater and reduce runoff. Permeable pavements allow water to infiltrate through them, capturing it for groundwater recharge. Green roofs, covered with vegetation, not only capture rainwater but also improve urban air quality and provide insulation.
- Solar-Powered Water Harvesting: Solar energy is increasingly being used to power water harvesting and purification systems. This approach is particularly beneficial in remote and off-grid areas. Solar panels can power pumps for groundwater extraction or provide energy

for desalination plants and AWGs, making water harvesting more sustainable and less dependent on traditional energy sources.

A Call to Action

The reality is that water scarcity is a pressing global issue. But with these challenges come opportunities, and the role of a water harvesting technician is one that promises both personal fulfilment and meaningful impact. By choosing a career in water management, you are becoming an agent of change in a world that desperately needs it.

Let's face it: water is life. It's the ultimate source of sustenance for all living beings. By preserving every precious drop, we safeguard our future and ensure the well-being of generations to come.

So, I implore you to embrace the possibilities that lie ahead. Take the knowledge you've gained from this chapter and let it inspire you to pursue a career that not only sustains you but sustains our planet as well. Become a water harvesting technician, and together, let's build a future where water scarcity is nothing more than a thing of the past.

Are you ready to make a difference?

7: Triumph In The Bicycle Repair Industry

No other invention combines business with pleasure as deeply as a bicycle.

Adam Opel

Sam knew uncertainty like an old friend. As a seasoned mechanic, his calloused hands told tales of battles with stubborn bolts and complex engines. But the recent scarcity of cars at Dan's Auto Repair shop was whispering a sobering narrative. Fuel prices were no longer a distant news headline; they were right there in the faces of his disappearing clientele. Could he become an outdated relic in an era transitioning away from gasoline?

The aroma of aged car parts and grease clung to the silent garage that normally thrummed with activity. Under the indifferent glow of flat fluorescent lights, Sam found himself alone with his worries, the persistent ticking of an old wall clock a monotonous soundtrack to his deep thoughts. How could he navigate this seemingly insurmountable tide of change?

In his shop-- a museum exhibit of an automotive era slowly but surely giving way to greener alternatives-- a lightbulb moment struck Sam. The looming end might just be a beckoning horizon ahead. As petroleum prices became monstrous, bicycles were re-emerging from the annals of nostalgic memories as the David against the Goliath of fossil fuel costs. Visions began to form in his mind's eye-- bicycle chains replacing fan belts, bicycle wheels replacing tire bearings.

The pump of adrenaline coursing through him was a cocktail of trepidation and thrill. He envisaged being huddled over a two-wheeler; fingers less grimy, tasks less bulky, yet equally as rewarding. There would be a learning essence to savour, a roadmap to sketch out for the seismic shift in direction, but he had faith in his long-nurtured mechanical skills.

As the setting sun painted the workshop walls soothing hues of deep orange, uncertainty clung onto Sam's mind again. Was it possible for him- an expert in hulking vehicle machinery- to adapt and cater to the delicate artistry of bicycles? Was he ready for a dual role of not just mending bikes but becoming an evangelist encouraging a greener path? It all seemed so monumental but within Sam, there was a kindle of determination, a drive that egged him on to register for a bicycle repair course.

As the dead quiet of the night wrapped around him, softening the sharp edges of his racing thoughts, Sam stood at a symbolical junction. Change was inevitable and he had to become a part of it-- resisting would only slow him down. His decision to switch his focus onto bicycles-- was this a desperate attempt to keep afloat, or had he unwittingly become an advocate pushing towards a sustainable future?

Pedalling for Change: Thriving in the Bicycle Repair Industry

Imagine a world where cars are no longer the primary modes of transportation. A world where the streets are filled with bicycles, the air filled with the hum of tires on asphalt, and the smiles of individuals who have found a sustainable way to get around. This may seem like a far-fetched vision, but as fuel prices continue to rise and people become more conscious of their environmental impact, the demand for alternative modes of transportation is steadily increasing.

In this chapter, we will explore the potential for growth and success in the bicycle repair industry. As more individuals turn to bicycles as a cost-effective and eco-friendly mode of transportation, the need for skilled bicycle repair and maintenance services will become paramount.

Recognizing the Potential Increase in Bicycle Usage

With fuel prices on the rise, many individuals are seeking out more affordable alternatives to driving a car. Bicycles offer a cost-effective option for daily commuting, as well as a fun and healthy way to get around town. As more people recognize the economic and environmental benefits of using bicycles, the demand for bike repair and maintenance services will undoubtedly increase.

Understanding the Importance of Bicycle Repair and Maintenance
Promoting sustainable transportation is essential for creating a more environmentally friendly future. By choosing bicycles over cars, individuals can reduce their carbon footprint and contribute to a greener planet. However, in order for bicycles to remain a viable mode of transportation, they need to be kept in proper working condition. This is where this industry comes in. Skilled technicians who understand the intricacies of bicycle maintenance and repair are vital for ensuring that bicycles remain a reliable and safe means of transportation.

Thrive in a Changing Economy

Learning the Skills and Knowledge Required for Success

Establishing a successful bicycle repair and maintenance service requires a combination of technical expertise and business acumen. In this chapter, we will delve into the skills and knowledge necessary to thrive in this industry. From understanding the components of a bicycle to developing customer service skills, we will provide a comprehensive guide for anyone interested in pursuing a career in this growing field.

A Roadmap to Success: Navigating the Bicycle Repair Industry

Goal: To provide a step-by-step process for establishing a successful bicycle repair and maintenance service.

1. Research and Market Analysis: Begin by researching the local market for bicycle repair services. Identify potential customers, competitors, and any niche markets that may exist. Evaluate the demand for these services and determine if there is a need for your skills and expertise.
2. Skill Development: Acquire the necessary technical skills and knowledge required to repair and maintain bicycles. This may involve attending a vocational school, enrolling in online courses, or apprenticing with an experienced bicycle repair technician.
3. Business Planning: Develop a comprehensive business plan that outlines your goals, target market, pricing strategy, marketing plan, and financial projections. Determine the start-up costs and secure any necessary funding.
4. Location and Equipment: Find a suitable location for your bicycle repair shop and equip it with the necessary tools and

equipment. Consider factors such as accessibility, foot traffic, and proximity to potential customers.
5. Marketing and Branding: Develop a strong brand identity and create a marketing strategy to attract customers. Utilise both online and offline marketing channels, such as social media, local advertising, and partnerships with local bike shops or organisations.
6. Customer Service and Satisfaction: Focus on providing outstanding customer service and ensuring customer satisfaction. Build relationships with customers, educate them about proper bicycle maintenance, and always go the extra mile to exceed their expectations.
7. Continuous Learning and Improvement: Stay up to date with the latest advancements in the bicycle repair industry. Attend workshops, conferences, and trade shows to expand your knowledge and skills. Continuously improve your services based on customer feedback and market trends.
8. Network and Collaboration: Build connections within the bicycle repair industry and collaborate with other professionals, such as bike shop owners and suppliers. Networking can lead to valuable partnerships and opportunities for growth.

By following this roadmap, you can establish a successful bicycle repair and maintenance service, contribute to a more sustainable future, and thrive in the changing economy. So, are you ready to pedal for change?

As fuel prices continue to rise and the environmental impact of cars becomes more apparent, individuals are increasingly seeking alternative modes of transportation. One such alternative that has gained popularity in recent years is the bicycle. Not only does cycling offer numerous health benefits, but it also provides a cost-effective and eco-friendly means of getting from point A to point B. As a result, there is a growing demand for bicycle repair and maintenance services.

Bicycles, like any mode of transportation, require regular maintenance to keep them in optimal condition. From fixing a flat tire to adjusting gears and brakes, pedal transport technicians play a crucial role in ensuring that cyclists can enjoy a smooth and safe ride. With the rise in bicycle usage, the demand for skilled bike repair professionals is bound to increase. Lookout for improved bike friendly infrastructure like:

- Protected Bike Lanes: Cities are increasingly installing physically separated bike lanes to protect cyclists from vehicular traffic. These lanes use barriers like curbs, planters, or parked cars to create a safe space for cycling. This separation significantly reduces the risk of collisions with motor vehicles.
- Advanced Stop Lines (ASLs) at Intersections: ASLs, also known as bike boxes, are designated areas at the front of traffic lights where cyclists can stop in full view of motorists. This increases the visibility of cyclists, especially at intersections, and reduces the risk of accidents like the right-hook collisions.
- Smart Traffic Signals: Some cities are implementing traffic lights that can detect bicycles and give them priority at intersections. These smart signals can adjust timings based on bike traffic, reducing wait times for cyclists and making cycling more efficient and safer in urban traffic.
- Bicycle Safety Education and Public Awareness Campaigns: Education for both cyclists and motorists about road safety, cycling laws, and mutual respect can significantly improve safety. Many cities have introduced

campaigns and programs to educate the public, fostering a more bike-friendly culture.
- Bike-Sharing Programs with Enhanced Safety Features: Modern bike-sharing programs often include bicycles equipped with safety features like automatic lights, robust brakes, and even GPS tracking. Some programs also offer helmets with rentals. These initiatives make cycling more accessible and safe for occasional riders or tourists who might not be familiar with the local biking environment.

By recognizing the potential increase in bicycle usage as an alternative to cars due to rising fuel prices, individuals can position themselves for success in this industry. Whether you are an aspiring technician looking to start your own repair shop or a cycling enthusiast looking to turn your passion into a career, there are ample opportunities for growth and success.

While the bicycle repair industry may not be as glamorous as other industries, it offers a level of stability and job security that many other professions cannot. As fuel prices continue to soar, more individuals will turn to bicycles as a practical and affordable means of transportation. This means that the demand for these services will only continue to grow.

By investing in the necessary skills and knowledge required to establish a successful bicycle repair and maintenance service, individuals can thrive in this changing economy. Whether you choose to pursue formal training or gain hands-on experience through apprenticeships or internships, there are various paths to success in this industry. The key is to stay ahead of the curve and continuously update your skills to meet the evolving needs of the cycling community.

Thrive in a Changing Economy

In conclusion, the rise in fuel prices and the move towards sustainable transportation options are driving the increased demand for bike repair and maintenance services. By recognizing the potential of bicycles as an alternative to cars and investing in the necessary skills, individuals can thrive in the bicycle repair industry. Whether you are an aspiring technician or a cycling enthusiast looking to turn your passion into a career, the opportunities for growth and success are vast. So, hop on your bike and join the ride towards a greener, healthier future.

Imagine a world where congested streets are a thing of the past, where the air is clean and free of emissions from cars, and where the simple act of riding a bicycle becomes a transformative force for change. This vision may seem idealistic, but it is not out of reach. In fact, with the rising fuel prices and the growing trend towards sustainable transportation, this future could be closer than you think.

Sustainable transportation is a hot topic these days, and for good reason. Cars contribute significantly to air pollution and greenhouse gas emissions, which are major contributors to climate change. As people become more conscious of their environmental impact, they are seeking alternative modes of transportation that are more eco-friendly. And that's where bicycles come in.

Bicycles are an incredibly efficient and sustainable means of transportation. They require no fuel other than the energy of the rider, making them a zero-emission mode of transport. They also take up far less space than cars, reducing congestion and making cities more livable. And let's not forget the health benefits of cycling – it's a great way to stay fit and active while getting from point A to point B.

But here's the thing: bicycles don't maintain themselves. Just like cars, they require regular maintenance and repair to keep them in good working order. And this is where the bicycle repair and maintenance industry comes in.

The bicycle repair and maintenance industry is an essential component of the sustainable transportation movement. By ensuring that bicycles are in proper working order, bike mechanics and technicians play a crucial role in promoting safe and efficient cycling. In doing so, they contribute to reducing the reliance on cars and promoting a more sustainable way of getting around.

So, what skills and knowledge are required to establish a successful bicycle repair and maintenance service? Well, first and foremost, you need a passion for bicycles. You need to understand how they work, how to identify and fix common problems, and how to keep them running smoothly. This requires a strong foundation in bicycle mechanics, which can be acquired through on-the-job training or formal education programs.

In conclusion, the bicycle repair and maintenance industry is a thriving and important part of the sustainable transportation movement. As more people turn to bicycles as a mode of transport, the demand for skilled bike mechanics and technicians will continue to grow. By embracing this growing trend and acquiring the necessary skills and knowledge, you can be a part of the solution and make a positive impact on the world. So, why not hop on your bike and pedal your way towards a career that is both rewarding and sustainable?

Are you someone who enjoys working with your hands and has a passion for bicycles? If so, then starting your own bicycle repair and maintenance service may be the perfect career path for you. As

Thrive in a Changing Economy

fuel prices continue to rise and personal car use declines, the demand for bicycles as a means of transportation is on the rise. And with that increase in bicycle usage comes a need for skilled technicians who can repair and maintain these valuable modes of transportation. In this section, we will explore the skills and knowledge required to establish a successful bicycle repair and maintenance service and how you can thrive in this expanding industry.

To begin, let's talk about the skills you will need to master in order to establish yourself in the bicycle repair industry. First and foremost, you will need a solid understanding of bicycle mechanics. This includes knowledge of how different bicycle components work, how to troubleshoot common issues, and how to perform repairs and maintenance tasks. This knowledge can be obtained through formal education programs, such as vocational or technical schools, or through hands-on experience working in a bicycle repair shop.

Additionally, you will need to develop strong problem-solving and critical thinking skills. Bicycles can be complex machines, and diagnosing and repairing issues often requires the ability to think logically and creatively. Being able to identify the root cause of a problem and develop an effective solution is crucial for success in this industry.

Now that we have discussed the necessary skills, let's shift our focus to the knowledge required to establish a successful bicycle repair and maintenance service. One key area of knowledge is business management. Starting your own business requires an understanding of basic accounting principles, marketing strategies, and customer relationship management. Obtaining this knowledge through formal education or by working closely with a mentor can help you navigate the unique challenges of running a small business.

Alongside business management knowledge, you will also need a sound understanding of bicycle industry trends and regulations. This includes staying aware of local and national laws pertaining to bicycles, as well as industry standards for safety and quality. By staying informed about these trends and regulations, you can ensure that you are providing a safe and compliant service to your customers.

In conclusion, establishing a successful bicycle repair and maintenance service requires a combination of technical skills, problem-solving abilities, and business management knowledge. By honing these skills and staying informed about industry trends, you can position yourself for success in the growing bicycle repair industry. So, if you're ready to make a change and start pedalling for change in a sustainable career, consider joining the ranks of bicycle repair technicians. With a passion for bicycles and the right skills and knowledge, you can thrive in this emerging field and contribute to a more sustainable future.

The bicycle repair industry is poised to thrive as the world shifts towards sustainable transportation options. With rising fuel prices and a growing awareness of the need to reduce our carbon footprint, bicycles are becoming a popular choice for many. As a result, the demand for bicycle repair and maintenance services is on the rise.

And it's not just about keeping bikes in working order. It's about promoting a sustainable future. By encouraging people to choose bicycles over cars, you're contributing to the reduction of greenhouse gas emissions and the preservation of our environment. It's a small step towards a bigger goal, but every little bit counts.

Imagine the satisfaction of seeing a well-loved bike brought back to life with your expert touch. Picture yourself working in a bright and bustling shop, surrounded by the buzz of customers excited to get their bikes back on the road. Smell the grease and hear the gentle hum of the tools as you work meticulously to ensure each bike is in optimal condition.

But that's not all. The bicycle repair industry offers more than just the satisfaction of a job well done. It also provides a flexible and fulfilling career path. Whether you choose to open your own repair shop or work for an established business, you'll have the freedom to set your own hours and be your own boss.

But I won't lie to you—it's not all sunshine and rainbows. Like any career, building a successful bicycle repair and maintenance service takes hard work, dedication, and a commitment to continuous learning. You'll need to stay up-to-date with the latest advances in bicycle technology and be able to adapt to changes in the industry.

But here's the thing: the rewards far outweigh the challenges. Not only will you enjoy the freedom and satisfaction that comes with running your own business, but you'll also be making a meaningful difference in the world. By promoting sustainable transportation and providing top-notch repair and maintenance services, you'll be helping to shape a greener future for all.

So, go ahead and take that leap. Embrace the potential of the bicycle repair industry and position yourself as a leader in this growing field. With rising fuel prices and a shifting mindset towards sustainability, the demand for your skills will only continue to rise. There has never been a better time to pedal your way to success in the bicycle repair world.

8: High Demand For Home Retrofitting Experts

You don't have to live in the country and grow your own food to be green.

Shalom Harlow

Radiating an air of quiet resolution, Roger was a man who tread thoughtfully on the earth. The whispers of a new era favouring eco-friendly practices resonated within him as he beheld his newly purchased ageing bungalow, ensconced among towering pines. His mind teemed with plans for an ambitious home retrofit, as images of insulation batts and double-glazed windows transformed into compelling ghost-like aspirations.

A strong gust of wind wove its prophetic message through the riotous colours of the autumn leaves, causing the old house's rickety windows to clatter. Cool tendrils of upcoming winter snaked through thin walls. Roger's hands found warmth deep inside the pockets of his weathered sweater, toying absentmindedly with an old coin—a tactile souvenir from times when fuel equated to excess and the concept of efficiency remained mostly uncharted.

His mind tiptoed back to a riveting lecture on the shifting economy. A charismatic speaker had heralded energy conservation as the currency of tomorrow. Standing in his barely furnished living room, Roger felt a resonant truth in those words. The future rested not on corporate giants but on vanguards of energy prudence, retrofitted homes, and individuals equipped with practical skills--each essential elements in a larger puzzle of sustainability. Names of various retrofitting experts swirled in his thoughts. He found himself musing aloud, "Who to reach out to first?" his question hanging in the room like an unresolved melody.

His sentimental grin faded as his fingers traced the draughty window frame, marking the gulf between his dreams and his current reality. The complexity of insulation was no longer just an intellectual consideration; it emerged as a challenge to his problem-solving abilities. The thought of window fitting loomed large—did he have the necessary aptitude and experience to master this skill, turning this energy-guzzling structure into a beacon of sustainable living?

Of course, he could. This wasn't theoretical physics. But his fretting didn't simply stem from changing his own living quarters. Every day brought growing demand for retrofitting specialists, hinting at a potential shift in his professional path—a path aligning perfectly with his principles and passion.

As the wind crooned its melancholy lullaby outside, Roger regarded his silent home, cradled by the forthcoming obstacles. He felt united with the burgeoning global movement towards energy efficiency. His readiness was apparent, but was the world prepared for this tide of change? More critically, how many were bracing the winter chill, oblivious to the dormant potential within their own homes to provide comforting warmth?

A Sustainable Future Starts at Home

Welcome to Chapter 8 of "Thrive in a Changing Economy: Alternative Careers for a Sustainable Future." In this chapter, we will delve into the world of home retrofitting and explore the demand for experts who can make homes more energy-efficient. As our understanding of climate change deepens and the urgent need for environmental sustainability becomes more apparent, the importance of energy-efficient homes cannot be overstated. But what exactly is home retrofitting, and why is it crucial in a changing economy? Let's find out.

Energy consumption in residential buildings accounts for a significant portion of our overall energy usage. In a changing economy where resources are becoming scarcer and more expensive, finding ways to reduce our energy consumption is not only environmentally responsible but also financially savvy. This is where home retrofitting comes into play. By making targeted improvements to existing homes, we can significantly enhance their energy efficiency and reduce the strain on our natural resources.

When we talk about home retrofitting, we are referring to a range of techniques and strategies aimed at improving the energy performance of a residence. These improvements can include insulation upgrades, window and door replacements, the installation of energy-efficient appliances, and the incorporation of renewable energy systems, among other things. By implementing these measures, homeowners can lower their energy bills, increase the comfort and livability of their homes, and contribute to a more sustainable future.

But how do we bring about these crucial changes? We need experts who possess the necessary skills and expertise in insulation and window fitting, among other areas, to carry out the retrofitting process. Individuals with a background in general handyman work are particularly well-suited for this field. By utilising their knowledge and craftsmanship, they can ensure that homes are properly sealed, preventing air leakage and minimising heat loss. These professionals play a vital role in improving residential energy efficiency and making homes more sustainable.

To excel as a home retrofitting expert, it is essential to develop a deep understanding of insulation materials and techniques, as well as window fitting methods. Insulation is like a cosy blanket that wraps around a home, keeping it warm in winter and cool in summer. By choosing the right materials and ensuring proper installation, you can make a significant impact on a home's energy efficiency. In the case of windows, these crucial openings can be a major source of energy loss if not properly sealed and insulated. Knowing how to install energy-efficient windows can make a substantial difference in a home's overall energy performance.

In this chapter, we will explore in detail the different aspects of home retrofitting and examine the specific skills and knowledge required to excel as a home retrofitting expert. We will dive into insulation materials and techniques, as well as the art of window fitting. With the global shift towards sustainable living and the increasing demand for energy-efficient homes, those with the expertise in home retrofitting will find themselves in high demand.

So, if you have a knack for handyman work, an eye for detail, and a passion for sustainability, this is the chapter for you. Join us as we uncover the world of home retrofitting, one nail and one window frame at a time. Together, we can build a more sustainable and energy-efficient future starting right in our own homes.

Energy-efficient homes are not only beneficial for the environment but also crucial in a changing economy. As we navigate the challenges of a rapidly evolving world, it becomes increasingly important to find sustainable solutions that can help us thrive. And one such solution lies in the retrofitting of homes to make them more energy-efficient.

Imagine a home that keeps you warm in the winter and cool in the summer, without relying heavily on heating or air conditioning systems. A home that reduces your energy bills and saves you money in the long run. A home that minimises your carbon footprint and contributes to a greener future. This is the essence of energy-efficient homes, and their significance cannot be overstated.

Energy-efficient homes offer numerous benefits, both to homeowners and the wider community. By reducing energy consumption, these homes help to conserve valuable resources, decrease greenhouse gas emissions, and mitigate the impacts of climate change. They also tackle the issue of rising energy costs, offering homeowners the opportunity to save money on their utility bills. In addition, energy-efficient homes improve indoor air quality, increase comfort levels, and enhance the overall quality of life for occupants.

While the concept of energy-efficient homes is not new, there is still much work to be done to make this a widespread reality. And this is where home retrofitting experts enter the stage. These professionals have the knowledge and skills to upgrade existing homes and make them more energy-efficient. From insulation to window fitting, they can identify areas of improvement and implement the necessary changes to maximise energy efficiency.

Home retrofitting is a powerful tool for improving residential energy efficiency. It involves assessing a home's current energy consumption, identifying areas of inefficiency, and implementing measures to address those issues. This can include insulating walls and attics, sealing air leaks, upgrading windows and doors, and installing energy-efficient appliances. By making these changes, homeowners can significantly reduce their energy usage and create a more sustainable living environment.

In a changing economy, the demand for home retrofitting experts is on the rise. As more homeowners recognize the importance of energy-efficient homes, there is a growing need for professionals who can provide the necessary expertise. Individuals with general handyman skills, especially in insulation and window fitting, will be in high demand as they help homeowners improve energy efficiency and contribute to a more sustainable future.

So, how can you become a part of this thriving field and provide vital home retrofitting services? Let's explore the different aspects of home retrofitting and its role in improving residential energy efficiency.

Home retrofitting is an essential aspect of improving residential energy efficiency and reducing our carbon footprint. By making simple modifications to our homes, we can significantly reduce energy consumption, lower utility bills, and create a more comfortable living environment. In this section, we will explore the different aspects of home retrofitting and how it plays a crucial role in creating sustainable homes.

One of the key components of home retrofitting is insulation. Proper insulation helps to maintain a consistent indoor temperature, reducing the need for excessive heating or cooling. By insulating walls, attics, and floors, homeowners can significantly reduce energy loss and improve energy efficiency. This not only saves money on utility bills but also reduces reliance on fossil fuels and lowers greenhouse gas emissions.

Another important aspect of home retrofitting is window fitting. Windows are a significant source of heat gain or loss, depending on the season. By installing energy-efficient windows, homeowners can reduce heat transfer and maintain a more comfortable indoor temperature. Energy-efficient windows are designed to minimise heat gain during hot summer months and prevent heat loss during cold winters. With proper window fitting, homeowners can reduce the strain on their HVAC systems, resulting in energy savings and improved sustainability.

Additionally, home retrofitting involves the installation of energy-efficient appliances and systems. Upgrading to energy-efficient HVAC systems, water heaters, and appliances can significantly reduce energy consumption. These systems are designed to use less energy while providing the same level of functionality. By investing in energy-efficient appliances, homeowners can save money and contribute to a more sustainable future.

Energy management systems and smart home technology also play a significant role in home retrofitting. These systems help homeowners monitor and control their energy usage, allowing for more efficient management. With the use of sensors, timers, and programmable thermostats, homeowners can optimise energy consumption, reduce waste, and improve overall efficiency. Smart home technology allows for remote control of various functions, enabling homeowners to easily manage and monitor their home's energy usage.

In conclusion, home retrofitting is crucial for improving residential energy efficiency and creating sustainable homes. By focusing on insulation, window fitting, energy-efficient appliances, and smart home technology, homeowners can significantly reduce energy consumption and lower their carbon footprint. Embracing these aspects of home retrofitting not only benefits the environment but also promotes energy savings and a more comfortable living environment. As the demand for energy-efficient homes continues to rise, individuals with expertise in home retrofitting will play a crucial role in meeting this demand and contributing to a sustainable future.

Insulation plays a significant role in reducing energy waste and maintaining optimal indoor temperatures. As a home retrofitting expert, your knowledge of insulation materials, their properties, and proper installation techniques will be crucial. Whether it's installing batt insulation in the walls, blown-in insulation in the attic, or foam insulation in crawl spaces, your expertise will ensure that homes maintain comfortable temperatures while minimising energy consumption.

Window fitting is another essential skill for home retrofitting experts. Windows are a significant source of heat gain or loss in a home, depending on the season. By properly fitting and sealing windows, you can prevent drafts, reduce energy loss, and contribute to overall climate control. Understanding the various types of windows, their energy efficiency ratings, and how to install them correctly will make you a valuable asset in the pursuit of energy-efficient homes.

Taking the initiative to gain expertise in insulation and window fitting will position you at the forefront of the demand for energy-efficient homes. As the emphasis on sustainability grows, homeowners will increasingly seek professionals who can help them reduce their ecological footprint while maximising energy efficiency. By honing your skills in these areas, you can thrive in a changing economy and contribute to a more sustainable future. The demand for home retrofitting experts will continue to rise, so it's time to acquire the necessary skills and expertise to excel in this rewarding career.

We've reached the end of this chapter, and I hope you now have a clear understanding of the demand for home retrofitting experts in our changing economy. Energy-efficient homes are becoming increasingly important as we face the challenges of climate change and the need to reduce our carbon footprint. As we've discussed, home retrofitting plays a vital role in improving residential energy efficiency, and individuals with general handyman skills, particularly in insulation and window fitting, will be in high demand to help make our homes more energy-efficient.

But why is this so important? Well the answer lies in the fact that our homes are one of the largest sources of energy consumption and greenhouse gas emissions. Just think about it: how many homes do you know that are draughty in the winter and sweltering hot in the summer? These are the homes that waste energy and contribute to the overall energy inefficiency of our society.

By retrofitting homes with proper insulation and energy-efficient windows, we can reduce energy consumption and lower carbon emissions. Imagine walking into a home that is cosy and warm in the winter, without any cold drafts sneaking in through the cracks. Picture a home where the summer heat stays outside, allowing you to enjoy a comfortable and cool indoor environment. Not only would these homes be more pleasant to live in, but they would also save homeowners a significant amount of money on their energy bills.

Here's the thing: the demand for energy-efficient homes and the expertise of home retrofitting professionals is only going to increase. As the focus on sustainability grows and governments implement stricter regulations to curb carbon emissions, homeowners will be looking for ways to improve the energy efficiency of their properties. And that's where you come in.

By acquiring the necessary skills and expertise in insulation and window fitting, you can position yourself as a sought-after home retrofitting expert. You will have the opportunity to make a real impact on the lives of homeowners while building a successful and rewarding career. Whether you choose to work independently or as part of a larger company, your skills will be in high demand, and you can be confident that your work is contributing to a more sustainable future.

Consider the possibilities that await you in the field of home retrofitting. With the right mix of passion, dedication, and technical know-how, you can play a pivotal role in creating energy-efficient homes for generations to come. Let's embrace this opportunity and work together to build a sustainable future, one home at a time. Keep up to date on the latest tech like:

- Smart Thermostats and Home Automation Systems: Modern smart thermostats learn from your habits and adjust heating and cooling for optimal energy use. Home automation systems can control lighting, heating, and appliances, maximizing energy efficiency and reducing costs.

- High-Performance Insulation: Advances in insulation materials, such as aerogel, vacuum insulated panels, and phase-change materials, offer superior thermal performance in a thinner profile. This makes them ideal for retrofitting existing homes where space for traditional insulation may be limited.
- Energy-Efficient Windows: Technological advancements in window design include triple-glazing, low-emissivity (low-E) coatings, and inert gas fills like argon or krypton between panes. These features significantly reduce heat transfer, helping to maintain a consistent indoor temperature and lower energy bills.
- Heat Pump Technology: Modern heat pumps are much more efficient than traditional heating systems and can provide both heating and cooling. Advances in this technology, such as ductless mini-split systems and geothermal heat pumps, offer high efficiency and lower operational costs, even in colder climates.
- Smart Water Systems: Advancements in water management technology for homes include smart water meters and leak detection systems. These systems use sensors and internet connectivity to monitor water usage in real-time, identify leaks early, and even shut off water supply in case of a major leak. This technology helps in conserving water, reducing wastage, and preventing damage from leaks, which is especially beneficial in older homes where plumbing issues might not be immediately apparent. Smart irrigation systems for gardens, which optimize water use based on weather forecasts and soil moisture levels, are also part of this advancement, contributing to more efficient and sustainable water use in residential settings.

Ready to take the next step? Let's dive into the next chapter, where we'll explore another exciting career opportunity in our changing economy. Until then, keep thinking green and remember that the power to make a difference lies in your hands.

9: Conquer The Art of Composting

After the Green Revolution, I came up with the concept of the Evergreen Revolution. In this we will see increase in farm productivity but without ecological harm.

M. S. Swaminathan

As the first light of dawn seeped into the night, painting the sky with soft hues of morning, Joe treaded lightly on dew-kissed grass towards his compost heap. The array of sprouting crops on his expansive farmland punctuated the rich soil like exclamations of hope. His hands, calloused and familiar with the honest toil of earth, sifted through churning mulch. A sigh hovered in stillness, somewhere between worry and satisfaction: his precious compost pile was dwindling.

Countless sunrises on the farm had taught Joe valuable truths. Chiefly, that waste was not just a discard from life's process but the very essence of renewal; a beautiful cycle that sustained his land and breathed life into his livelihood.

An echo from the past, an old documentary about sustainable agriculture, seemed suddenly vibrant in Joe's memory. Its message had been simple and sublime: using waste as a catalyst for fertility rather than a pollutant. Despite the allure, it had been an abstract dream back then; embryonic and demanding faith to become tangible.

Moving past points of contemplation, Joe recognized his challenge and its solution were one in the same—composting. Memories of mounting piles of organic waste from city markets flooded back, now with the potential of life-giving nutrition. Achieving perfect harmony between nitrogen and carbon seemed a daunting task, almost like choreographing an intricate ballet for elements of nature. But the prospect kindled something primal within him; a legacy of his pioneers and a voice from the land he nurtured.

In the comforting solitude of his rustic kitchen, under the flickering glow of a stove's warmth, he started building bridges across this knowledge gap about composting. He navigated complex charts and diagrams without losing heart, his hardened farmer's hands turning pages with reverent determination. Slowly, he started to comprehend this silent dialect spoken through the rustling leaves and the relentless journey of earthworms - a language of life, bloom, and decay. Composting was more than a waste management solution—it was a gentle rhythm pulsating in the heart of earth, an endless cycle of new beginnings.

His gaze lingered on a framed photograph of his forefathers—stern faces peering above faded overalls. They, too, had been nurtured by this earth, and had ploughed the same fields he did. A new question began to frolic in his mind: could he follow the footsteps of his ancestors? Could he decode this mysterious rhythm of the soil to transform what seems rejected into a source of robust growth?

Unlocking the Hidden Potential of Organic Waste

As we continue to navigate an ever-changing global landscape, it has become abundantly clear that sustainable practices are not just a luxury, but a necessity. In order to build a resilient future, we must explore alternative careers that promote sustainability and address the pressing challenges facing our environment. One such career that holds immense potential is that of a composting specialist. In this chapter, we will delve into the art of composting and discover how these specialists play a vital role in transforming organic waste into nutrient-rich soil.

Sustainable Waste Management: A Cornerstone of Agriculture and Gardening

Before we can truly appreciate the importance of composting, it is essential to understand the significance of sustainable waste management in agriculture and gardening. Organic waste, such as food scraps and yard trimmings, has long been viewed as a burden to be disposed of. However, this mindset fails to recognize the immense value that lies within these materials. By diverting organic waste from landfills and harnessing its potential, we can create a closed-loop system that benefits both the environment and our food systems.

Composting specialists are key players in this process, working to transform organic waste into valuable compost through the natural decomposition of organic materials. By taking this waste and turning it into a valuable resource, composting specialists are able to contribute to the sustainability of our agricultural and gardening practices. By enriching the soil with essential nutrients, compost not only improves crop yields but also reduces the need for harmful chemical fertilisers. Thus, by embracing sustainable waste management, we can create a symbiotic relationship between organic waste and the cultivation of healthy, nutritious food.

The Art of Composting: Transforming Waste into Wealth

So how does one transform organic waste into valuable compost? The process may seem simple on the surface, but it requires knowledge, skill, and a touch of artistry. **Composting specialists understand the delicate balance required to facilitate the decay of organic materials**. They carefully layer green and brown waste, ensuring a harmonious blend of nitrogen-rich materials like grass clippings and fruit scraps, and carbon-rich materials like dead leaves and wood chips. This delicate balance creates the optimal environment for beneficial microorganisms to thrive, breaking down the organic matter and transforming it into humus - the magic ingredient that grants compost its extraordinary properties.

As composting specialists guide this transformation, they must also be attuned to the needs of the compost pile. **Just like a conductor leading an orchestra, they must monitor temperature, moisture levels, and the presence of oxygen**. These elements, when managed correctly, contribute to the overall health and vitality of the compost pile. By creating the ideal conditions, composting specialists can accelerate the decomposition process, producing high-quality compost in a shorter amount of time.

Cultivating Skills for Success in Composting

Becoming a successful composting specialist requires a unique set of skills and techniques. While formal education may not be a prerequisite, a passion for sustainability and a deep understanding of the composting process are essential. **Composting specialists must possess knowledge in organic waste management, plant biology, and environmental science**. This expertise allows them to troubleshoot common challenges, such as odours or pest infestations, and make informed decisions on how to rectify these issues.

Moreover, **attention to detail and a love for experimentation are key traits of a successful composting specialist**. They must have the patience and curiosity to fine-tune their composting recipe, tweaking proportions and ratios to achieve the desired results. Like alchemists, they constantly seek the perfect formula that transforms waste into wealth.

In addition to these technical skills, composting specialists must also possess excellent communication and outreach abilities. They often work with local communities, educating them on the benefits of composting and providing guidance on how to implement composting practices at home or in their businesses. By empowering others to embrace sustainable waste management, composting specialists not only contribute to the health of our soils but also foster a culture of environmental stewardship.

Embracing the Transformative Power of Composting

In Chapter 9 of "Thrive in a Changing Economy: Alternative Careers for a Sustainable Future," we have explored the invaluable role of composting specialists in sustainable waste management and the cultivation of nutrient-rich soil. As the world continues to confront the pressing challenges of climate change and food security, the demand for these professionals will only grow. By unlocking the hidden potential within organic waste, composting specialists have the power to shape a future where waste is transformed into wealth, and our soils and food systems thrive. So let us embrace the art of composting and embark on a journey towards a more sustainable and abundant tomorrow.

Sustainable waste management is a critical component of agriculture and gardening. As we strive to create a more sustainable future, it is important to recognize that waste is not simply something to be disposed of, but rather a valuable resource that can be transformed into nutrient-rich soil. By understanding the importance of composting and sustainable waste management, we can contribute to the growth and health of our gardens and agricultural systems.

Organic waste, such as food scraps and yard trimmings, makes up a significant portion of the waste stream. When this waste is sent to landfills, it decomposes anaerobically, releasing harmful greenhouse gases such as methane. However, when properly managed and composted, this waste can be transformed into a valuable soil amendment. Composting not only diverts waste from landfills, but also reduces the need for synthetic fertilisers and provides a natural alternative for improving soil health.

Composting is a natural process that has been used for centuries to recycle organic materials. Through this process, organic waste is broken down by microorganisms such as bacteria, fungi, and earthworms, resulting in a nutrient-rich compost. This compost can be used to enrich soil, improve plant growth, and increase water retention.

Successful composting requires careful management of the compost pile, including monitoring temperature, moisture levels, and the carbon-to-nitrogen ratio. Understanding these factors and how they affect the decomposition process is essential for producing high-quality compost. Additionally, different types of organic materials can be composted, including food scraps, yard waste, and even animal manure. By composting these materials, we can not only reduce waste, but also create a valuable resource for our gardens and farms. Sometimes, we take waste for granted whilst it can be turned into something valuable.

Composting specialists play a crucial role in managing and transforming organic waste into a valuable resource. These individuals have a deep understanding of the composting process and can effectively manage compost piles to produce high-quality compost. They may work for municipalities, farms, or gardening centres, helping to divert waste from landfills and promote sustainable practices. Composting specialists may also educate others about the benefits of composting and provide resources for individuals and communities to compost their own waste.

As we move towards a more sustainable future, the need for composting specialists will only continue to grow. These individuals will be instrumental in transforming organic waste into valuable compost and promoting sustainable waste management practices. Whether you are a gardener looking to improve the health of your soil or someone interested in a career in sustainable waste management, understanding the importance of composting is essential. So, let's explore the process of transforming organic waste into valuable compost and learn the skills and techniques required to become a successful composting specialist. By doing so, we can contribute to a more sustainable and thriving future.

Let's explore the art of composting and uncover the secrets of nutrient-rich soil.

Composting is like a magical process that, with the right ingredients and conditions, transforms ordinary organic waste into a valuable resource. It's like taking a pile of discarded materials and turning them into a vibrant ecosystem that nourishes plants and enriches the soil. Imagine creating a symphony of nutrients that invigorates the earth, one compost pile at a time.

So how does this transformation of waste into treasure actually happen? It all starts with the right ingredients. Like a chef selecting the finest ingredients for a gourmet meal, a composting specialist carefully chooses the organic matter that will make up the compost pile. This can include fruit and vegetable scraps, coffee grounds, eggshells, leaves, grass clippings, and even shredded paper. It's a symphony of waste that will soon become a nutrient-rich masterpiece.

Once the ingredients are gathered, it's time to create the compost pile. Like a sculptor shaping a work of art, the composting specialist assembles the materials in layers, ensuring a balance of carbon-rich "browns" and nitrogen-rich "greens." These browns, such as dried leaves or wood chips, provide carbon, while the greens, like fresh grass clippings or kitchen scraps, supply nitrogen. It's a delicate dance of proportions and ratios, with the composting specialist as the conductor, guiding the process.

But the transformation doesn't stop there. Like a gardener tending to a flourishing garden, the composting specialist must provide the right environment for the organic matter to break down and decompose. This means maintaining the optimal moisture levels, turning the pile regularly to aerate it, and ensuring a good balance of air and water. It's a continuous process of observation and adjustment, where the composting specialist is like an artist, constantly refining their masterpiece.

As the compost pile undergoes its magical transformation, microorganisms, insects, and earthworms all play their part. Like an orchestra of tiny creatures, they break down the organic matter, converting it into humus, a dark, crumbly substance that resembles chocolate cake crumbs. This humus is teeming with beneficial bacteria and fungi that improve soil structure, retain moisture, and release essential nutrients to plants. It's like giving the earth a nourishing feast.

So why is all of this important? Well, composting not only reduces the amount of waste going into landfills but also mitigates greenhouse gas emissions. It helps to build healthy soil, reduces the need for synthetic fertilisers, and ultimately promotes sustainable agriculture and gardening practices. By becoming a composting specialist, you can be a part of this transformative process and contribute to a more sustainable future.

The art of composting is a skill that is becoming increasingly important in our quest for sustainable waste management and soil fertility. Composting specialists are individuals who have mastered the techniques of transforming organic waste into valuable compost that can be used in agriculture and gardening. By developing these skills, composting specialists play a crucial role in reducing waste, improving soil health, and contributing to a more sustainable future.

In addition to scientific knowledge, composting specialists need practical skills in managing compost piles. They must be able to properly mix and turn organic materials to ensure adequate aeration and moisture levels. This involves knowing the right ratios of carbon-rich (browns) and nitrogen-rich (greens) materials, as well as the optimal moisture content for decomposition. Specialists also need to monitor temperature and adjust the compost pile as needed to maintain optimal conditions for decomposition.

A successful composting specialist also knows the importance of troubleshooting and problem-solving. Composting is not always a straightforward process, and issues such as foul odours, pests, or slow decomposition can occur. Specialists need to be able to identify the cause of these problems and implement solutions to remedy them. This may involve adjusting the carbon-to-nitrogen ratio, addressing moisture imbalances, or introducing beneficial organisms to the compost pile.

Furthermore, a composting specialist must have knowledge of different composting systems and techniques. There are various methods to choose from, including traditional composting, vermicomposting (using worms), and bokashi composting (fermentation). Each method has its own benefits and considerations, and specialists need to be proficient in their application. They must also stay updated on new advancements and emerging technologies in composting to continuously improve their skills and knowledge. Keep informed on latest advances in composting like:

- In-Vessel Composting Systems: These systems allow for greater control over environmental conditions like temperature, moisture, and aeration within a closed container. In-vessel composting accelerates the composting process, reduces odor, and can handle a wide range of

organic waste materials, making it suitable for urban and industrial settings.
- Aerated Static Pile Composting: This method involves layering organic waste with a bulking agent like wood chips to allow air flow. It's then equipped with a system of pipes to inject air into or draw air out of the pile, enhancing aerobic decomposition. This method is more space-efficient and less labor-intensive than traditional composting methods, making it ideal for larger-scale operations.
- Anaerobic Digestion: This technology breaks down organic matter in the absence of oxygen, producing biogas that can be used to generate electricity or heat. The remaining material can be used as a fertilizer. Anaerobic digestion is highly efficient for handling food waste and other organic materials and is increasingly being adopted in urban and industrial waste management systems.
- Compostable Plastics Breakdown: Advances in composting technologies have led to the development of methods capable of breaking down certified compostable plastics. These plastics are designed to decompose in industrial composting facilities, offering a solution for the disposal of plastic packaging in a more environmentally friendly way.
- Community and Urban-Scaled Composting Initiatives: There's a growing trend in implementing community-based and urban-scaled composting programs. These programs focus on local waste collection and processing, reducing transportation costs and emissions associated with waste management. They often use innovative models like decentralized composting hubs, which can process waste from local sources more efficiently and support community gardens or urban agriculture projects.

In conclusion, the skills and techniques required to become a successful composting specialist are varied and multifaceted. It requires a combination of scientific knowledge, practical skills, troubleshooting abilities, and a passion for sustainability. By mastering these skills, composting specialists can make a significant impact in waste management, soil fertility, and sustainable agriculture and gardening practices. They are the heroes of the composting world, transforming organic waste into valuable compost and paving the way for a greener future.

The Future is in Your Hands

As we conclude this chapter on the art of composting, it becomes clear that sustainable waste management is critical to the future of agriculture and gardening. The transformation of organic waste into valuable compost is not just a noble endeavour, but a necessary one for our ever-changing economy. And who better to take on this important task than composting specialists?

Composting specialists are poised to play a crucial role in the management and transformation of organic waste into a valuable resource. With their expertise and skills, they have the power to make a significant impact on the sustainability of our environment and the success of local agriculture.

But what does it take to become a successful composting specialist? It requires a deep understanding of the composting process, from the science behind it to the techniques and skills needed to execute it effectively. It also requires a passion for sustainability and an unwavering commitment to making a difference.

The Art and Science of Composting

Composting is both an art and a science. It involves the careful balance of organic materials, moisture levels, and oxygen to create the optimal conditions for decomposition. It requires knowledge of the different types of organic waste and how they interact with one another in the composting process. It calls for a keen eye and a sense of intuition to know when the compost is ready for use.

As a composting specialist, you will learn to navigate this delicate ecosystem of organic waste. You will become familiar with the different composting methods, from traditional outdoor piles to more modern approaches like vermicomposting and aerated static pile composting. You will gain the skills to diagnose and troubleshoot common issues that may arise during the composting process, ensuring that the compost remains healthy and productive.

From Waste to Wealth

Transforming organic waste into valuable compost is not just about reducing landfill waste. It's about turning what was once considered useless into something incredibly valuable. Think of it as a magical alchemy, where scraps and leftovers are transformed into fertile soil, feeding and nourishing the plants that sustain us all.

Imagine walking through a lush garden, each plant bursting with vibrancy and vitality. You can feel the rich, loamy soil under your feet, see the colourful blooms dancing in the breeze, and smell the earthy aroma that can only come from thriving, nutrient-rich soil. This is the world that composting specialists create through their dedicated work.

A Collaborative Effort

Becoming a successful composting specialist is not a solitary journey. It requires collaboration and partnerships with local gardeners, farmers, and community organisations. By working together, we can create a sustainable and resilient food system that benefits both the environment and our communities.

As a composting specialist, you have the opportunity to make a real difference in your local community. You can educate and inspire others to adopt sustainable waste management practices, and in turn, help them produce healthier crops and gardens. Through your expertise, you can empower individuals and communities to take control of their own food production, creating a more sustainable and self-reliant future.

A Sustainable Future Beckons

The future is calling, and it's a future that embraces sustainability and responsible waste management. Composting specialists have a unique and essential role to play in shaping this future. By transforming organic waste into valuable compost, they not only help reduce landfill waste but also create a resource that enriches the soil, nourishes plants, and sustains our communities.

As we move forward, let us remember the power of composting. Let us celebrate the art and science behind it, and let us honour the dedicated composting specialists who are transforming waste into wealth. Together, we can build a future that is not only environmentally sustainable but also economically prosperous. The choice is in our hands, and the time to act is now.

Thrive in a Changing Economy

10: Bloom Off The Beaten Track

As consumers, we have so much power to change the world by just being careful in what we buy.

Emma Watson

Beneath the metallic lattice of a highway overpass, Roger held his post against a backdrop of coal-dusted walls and the mirror-like skyscrapers downtown. An isolated silhouette in the subdued light of dusk, he possessed an "Open" sign that flickers intermittently, defiantly challenging the thickening night. From noon until midnight, he oversaw his modest second-hand enterprise, his collection of well-loved trinkets, clothes and tools arrayed on the humble concrete stage beneath his feet. His eyes saw beauty in the discarded, practicality in the abandoned, and potential in the matchless homes yet to cherish these items.

As each car and person moved by, a relentless machine consumed fresh commodities, yet Roger stood resolute amidst it all. He wasn't a protestor or a cynic; instead, he was an optimist, believing fervently in the value of giving things a second life. The concern for sustainable consumption wasn't an invading threat but rather a shimmering beacon, signalling boundless opportunities on the horizon.

A mélange of smells - rusted metal, worn-out leather and prints from a bygone era – played with Roger's senses in the cool evening breeze. The patchwork display was more than just old items—it was a mosaic of personal histories and forgotten moments. Each object held a silent whisper of its past, awaiting another story to be written. His stand wasn't merely a business; it embodied Roger's raison d'être. He resuscitated dreams and memories through forgotten treasures, making a canvas out of his humble second-hand market.

As the twilight hour swept in bringing darker shadows that capered across the scattered wares, the horizon blazed with streaks of crimson and amber – the day's final salute. Life whirled around him in its unending rhythm. The city's artificial lights began to twinkle amidst the gathering darkness. Off to one side, the laughter of children echoed, prying Roger away from his world of dreams and back to reality. His dreams and the real world existed together, a tango of what was and what could be.

His gaze returned to his unexpected haven beneath the overpass, teeming with discarded relics reborn as dreams. Roger cherished the satisfied smiles, softened gazes, and heartfelt thanks that came from customers as they discovered his carefully curated treasurers. The world did not stop for Roger's second-hand dreams, nor did his reveries pause for the world's ceaseless march—both lived side by side in a tender dance of reality and possibility. Marrying the past with the present, he breathed a new life into forsaken artefacts.

Can such moments of fulfilment also suggest the sprouting of a fresh trend toward sustainable consumption and tangible evidence of burgeoning careers in the second-hand goods market?

The Second-Hand Market: A Thriving Opportunity in a Changing Economy

In our ever-changing world, one thing is certain: the demand for goods continues to grow. However, as the availability of new goods declines and their prices rise, consumers are searching for more affordable and sustainable alternatives. This is where the second-hand market comes into play. From clothing to tools, the demand for quality second-hand items is on the rise, presenting a unique opportunity for those looking to thrive in a changing economy.

The second-hand market offers a wide range of career possibilities. As more people become conscious of their environmental impact and seek to reduce waste, they are turning to second-hand goods as a sustainable choice. This shift in consumer behaviour opens up avenues for entrepreneurs and professionals to provide high-quality, pre-owned products to meet the growing demand.

One area where the second-hand market is booming is in the fashion industry. As the climate crisis gains more attention and concern, consumers are reevaluating their shopping habits and turning away from fast fashion. Instead, they are opting for gently used clothing and accessories, which not only reduces waste but also allows for unique and individual styles. This presents an opportunity for second-hand clothing stores and online platforms to thrive and cater to the needs of conscious consumers.

Another sector within the second-hand market that is flourishing is the resale of electronics and technology. With the constant release of new gadgets and devices, consumers are looking for ways to upgrade without breaking the bank. This has created a thriving market for refurbished electronics, where professionals can repair and resell previously owned devices at a fraction of the cost of new ones. This not only provides affordable options for consumers but also reduces electronic waste and promotes resource optimization.

In addition to fashion and electronics, the second-hand market offers opportunities in various other industries. Home goods, furniture, books, and even tools are all in high demand as people seek to furnish their homes and live sustainably. By recognizing these growing consumer needs, individuals can tap into the second-hand market and create thriving careers.

The importance of sustainable consumption and resource optimization cannot be overstated. As our global resources become more limited, it is crucial that we find ways to make the most of what we have. By choosing to buy second-hand goods, we reduce the demand for new products and extend the lifespan of existing ones. This not only benefits the environment but also helps individuals and communities save money and become more resilient in an uncertain economy.

In conclusion, the second-hand market presents a unique opportunity for individuals looking to thrive in a changing economy. By recognizing the growing demand for affordable and sustainable second-hand goods, exploring potential careers in the second-hand market, and understanding the importance of sustainable consumption and resource optimization, individuals can carve out successful and fulfilling paths for themselves. As we navigate the challenges of a changing economy, the second-hand market offers a promising future for those who are willing to embrace the opportunity.

Growing Your Second-Hand Business: A Step-by-Step Guide to Success

The second-hand market offers a world of possibilities for entrepreneurs and professionals. Whether you're considering starting a second-hand clothing store or venturing into the resale of electronics, it's important to have a well-defined plan to guide your path to success. Here is a step-by-step process to help you grow your second-hand business and take advantage of the opportunities in this thriving market.

1. **Define your niche**: The second-hand market is vast and diverse, so it's essential to narrow down your focus and identify your target audience. Decide what type of second-hand goods you want to specialise in and understand the needs and preferences of your potential customers. By defining your niche, you can tailor your products and services to meet the specific demands of your market.
2. **Source quality products**: To build a successful second-hand business, you need a steady supply of high-quality products. Develop relationships with suppliers, establish partnerships with individuals, and explore online platforms where you can find pre-owned items that meet your standards. Make sure to thoroughly inspect and assess the condition of each item to ensure its resale value.
3. **Create a compelling brand**: In a competitive market, a strong brand will set you apart from the crowd. Define your brand identity and communicate your values to attract like-minded customers. Whether you're focused on sustainability, affordability, or unique fashion, make sure your branding aligns with your target audience's preferences and aspirations.

4. **Build an online presence**: In today's digital age, an online presence is crucial for business success. Create a visually appealing website or set up shop on online marketplaces to reach a wider audience. Utilise social media platforms to showcase your products, engage with customers, and build a community around your brand. Invest in search engine optimization to improve your online visibility and attract organic traffic.
5. **Provide exceptional customer service**: Building strong relationships with your customers is key to growing your second-hand business. Offer excellent customer service, respond to inquiries promptly, and provide accurate and detailed product descriptions. Consistently deliver on your promises and go the extra mile to exceed customer expectations. Positive word-of-mouth can be a powerful tool for attracting new customers.
6. **Market strategically**: Develop a marketing strategy that aligns with your target audience's preferences and behaviours. Utilise both online and offline marketing channels to reach your potential customers. Consider hosting events, collaborating with influencers or fashion bloggers, and partnering with local organisations to increase brand awareness and attract new customers.
7. **Continuously adapt and improve**: The second-hand market is constantly evolving, so it's essential to stay on top of trends and adapt your business accordingly. Monitor consumer preferences, keep an eye on industry developments, and be open to feedback from your customers. Continuously evaluate and improve your products, services, and processes to stay ahead of the competition and provide the best possible experience for your customers.

8. **Measure success and adjust**: Set measurable goals for your second-hand business and regularly assess your progress. Monitor key performance indicators such as sales volume, customer satisfaction, and online engagement. Use analytics tools to gain insights into consumer behaviour and adjust your strategies accordingly. Celebrate your successes, learn from your failures, and always strive for continuous improvement.

Follow this step-by-step process to chart a path to success in the second-hand market. Take advantage of the growing demand for affordable and sustainable goods, and turn your passion for reuse and resource optimization into a thriving and fulfilling career. With dedication, creativity, and a customer-centric approach, you can build a successful second-hand business and make a positive impact in a changing economy.

Tool Librarian

Start a successful Tool Library or become a Sharing Economy Coordinator involves careful planning and execution. Here's a step-by-step guide:

- Research the Market: Understand the local demand for a tool library. Identify what tools and equipment people most commonly need but may not own.
- Develop a Business Plan: Outline your mission, operational strategy, financial projections, and marketing plans. Consider aspects like membership fees, rental charges, and funding sources.
- Secure Funding: Explore various funding options such as grants, donations, crowdfunding, sponsorships, or loans. Community support can be vital in this stage.

- Choose a Suitable Location: Find a convenient, accessible, and safe location for your tool library. Consider factors like storage space, parking, and ease of access for members.
- Acquire Tools and Equipment: Source your inventory through purchases, donations, or partnerships. Start with a basic set of commonly used tools and expand as demand grows.
- Implement a Tracking System: Invest in or develop a tool tracking system to manage inventory, rentals, check-ins, and check-outs efficiently.
- Set Up a Membership System: Create a membership structure with clear terms and conditions. Include aspects like rental policies, late fees, and member responsibilities.
- Develop Safety and Usage Guidelines: Provide clear guidelines and possibly training for the safe and proper use of tools. This step is crucial for liability and user safety.
- Hire and Train Staff: If needed, hire and train staff or volunteers to manage the tool library and assist members.
- Establish Partnerships: Collaborate with local businesses, community organizations, and schools to increase your reach and resources.
- Launch a Marketing Campaign: Use social media, local events, flyers, and community networks to promote your tool library and attract members.
- Organize Community Events: Host workshops, tool demonstrations, and community projects to engage members and promote the sharing economy concept.
- Gather Feedback: Regularly collect feedback from members to understand their needs and improve services.
- Ensure Compliance and Insurance: Make sure your operation complies with local regulations and has appropriate insurance to cover liabilities.

- Evaluate and Adapt: Continuously assess the performance of your tool library and adapt your strategy, inventory, and services to meet evolving community needs.

Carpool Coordinator

Start a successful business as a Carpool Coordinator with strategic planning, understanding local transportation needs, and effective communication. Balance logistical planning with a strong focus on community engagement and user experience. Keep abreast of local transportation needs and trends to ensure your service remains relevant and valuable.

Here are 11 steps to guide you through this process:

- Conduct Market Research: Understand the commuting patterns, traffic issues, and public transportation gaps in your target area. Identify potential carpoolers like corporate employees, students, or residents in suburban areas.
- Develop a Business Plan: Outline your business model, target market, pricing strategy, and growth projections. Decide whether your service will be app-based, web-based, or both.
- Secure Funding: Depending on your scale, you might need funding for technology development, marketing, and operations. Consider options like loans, grants, or investors.
- Develop a Platform: Create a user-friendly website or mobile app where users can register, create profiles, schedule rides, and manage payments. Ensure robust privacy and security measures.
- Set Policies and Guidelines: Establish clear policies for ride scheduling, cancellations, payments, vehicle standards, and user conduct. This includes safety protocols and COVID-19 precautions, if applicable.

- Obtain Necessary Permits and Insurance: Ensure you have the necessary business permits and liability insurance to operate legally and protect your business.
- Build a Network of Drivers: Recruit drivers who have reliable vehicles and clean driving records. Conduct background checks and vehicle inspections for safety.
- Launch Marketing Campaigns: Use social media, local advertisements, partnerships with businesses and institutions, and community events to promote your carpooling service.
- Implement a Pricing Structure: Decide on your pricing model – whether it's a subscription fee, per-ride charge, or a commission-based system. Ensure it's competitive yet sustainable.
- Offer Customer Support: Provide reliable customer service to handle inquiries, complaints, and assistance. This can include a helpdesk, chat support, or a hotline.
- Evaluate and Adapt: Continuously gather feedback from users to improve your service. Stay adaptable to changing market needs, technological advancements, and transportation trends.

Greenhouse Guide

Start a successful business as a Greenhouse Erector, Maintenance Engineer, and Operator Trainer with a combination of technical expertise, business acumen, and teaching skills. This business requires balancing technical expertise with strong project management and customer service skills. Here are 14 steps to guide you through the process:

- Acquire Necessary Skills and Knowledge: Ensure you have in-depth knowledge of greenhouse construction, maintenance, and operation. Consider formal education or training in horticulture, engineering, or related fields.
- Conduct Market Research: Understand the needs of your potential clients, such as commercial farmers, educational institutions, or research centers. Identify the types of greenhouses in demand and the services most needed.
- Develop a Business Plan: Outline your services, target market, competition, pricing strategy, and growth projections. Include plans for marketing, staffing, and financial management.
- Secure Funding: Depending on your scale, you may need funding for tools, equipment, vehicles, and initial operating costs. Consider options like business loans, grants, or investors.
- Obtain Certifications and Licenses: Acquire any necessary certifications or licenses that demonstrate your expertise and comply with local regulations.
- Purchase Tools and Equipment: Invest in high-quality tools and equipment for greenhouse erection and maintenance. Consider also investing in technology for design and project management.
- Hire Skilled Staff: If needed, hire staff with experience in construction, engineering, or horticulture. Ensure they have or receive proper training.
- Establish Supplier Relationships: Build relationships with suppliers of greenhouse materials and equipment. Consider partnerships for better pricing or exclusive materials.

- Develop Training Programs: Create comprehensive training programs for greenhouse operators, covering topics like structure maintenance, climate control, and plant management.
- Market Your Services: Use a mix of online and offline marketing strategies to reach your target audience. This can include a website, social media, attending trade shows, and networking with industry professionals.
- Implement a Safety Protocol: Ensure all work complies with safety standards. This includes training staff in safety practices and equipping them with necessary safety gear.
- Offer Customized Solutions: Provide tailored services to meet the specific needs of your clients. This could involve custom greenhouse designs or specialized maintenance plans.
- Set Up an Efficient Operational Workflow: Develop efficient processes for project management, from initial consultations to construction, maintenance, and training.
- Gather Feedback and Adapt: Regularly solicit feedback from clients to improve your services. Stay updated with the latest greenhouse technologies and practices to keep your business competitive.

Craft a Career as a Local Artisan

Start up as a local artisan by honing your craft and also your business and marketing acumen. Remember, the key to success as a local artisan is not just in creating beautiful or unique items, but also in effectively managing the business side of your art. Stay true to your artistic vision while being adaptable to market trends and customer feedback. Here are nine steps to guide you:

Thrive in a Changing Economy

- Develop Your Artisan Skills: Focus on perfecting your craft, whether it's pottery, woodworking, jewelry making, or another form of art. Consider taking workshops or classes to refine your techniques and learn new ones.
- Identify Your Niche: Determine what makes your work unique. Understanding your style and what sets you apart in the market can help you target the right audience.
- Create a Business Plan: Outline your business goals, target market, pricing strategy, production costs, and potential revenue streams. A well-thought-out plan is crucial for a successful business.
- Build a Portfolio: Develop a collection of your work to showcase your skills and style. This portfolio can be physical or digital, like a website or social media profile.
- Set Up a Workshop or Studio: Establish a space where you can work efficiently. Ensure it has the necessary tools and materials, and consider its accessibility for potential clients or visitors.
- Develop a Brand and Online Presence: Create a brand that reflects your art and personality. Set up a website and social media accounts to showcase your work, share your creative process, and connect with customers and other artists.
- Market Your Art: Attend local art fairs, exhibitions, and craft shows to showcase your work. Consider selling online through platforms like Etsy, or your own website. Collaborate with local businesses or galleries to reach a wider audience.
- Network with Other Artisans and Artists: Building relationships with other artists can provide support, inspiration, and opportunities for collaboration. Join local art associations or online communities.

- Manage Your Finances: Keep track of your income and expenses. Understand the basics of bookkeeping, and consider using software to help with this. It's also wise to set aside money for taxes and unforeseen expenses.

Local wildlife conservation coordinator

A local wildlife conservation project manager has a blend of environmental knowledge, project management skills, and community engagement tact. They rely heavily building strong relationships with various stakeholders and maintaining flexibility in your approach. Here are nine steps to guide you through the process:

- Gain Relevant Knowledge and Experience: Obtain a solid foundation in wildlife conservation, ecology, or a related field through education or practical experience. Understanding local wildlife and ecosystems is crucial.
- Identify Conservation Needs and Opportunities: Research the local environment to identify key wildlife conservation needs and opportunities. This could involve species protection, habitat restoration, or community education.
- Develop a Detailed Plan: Outline your conservation goals, strategies, and timelines. This plan should include specific projects, such as habitat restoration, species monitoring, or public education campaigns.
- Secure Funding and Resources: Explore funding sources such as grants, donations, government funding, or partnerships with NGOs. You'll also need to consider resources like equipment, field supplies, and possibly office space.
- Build a Network of Partners and Volunteers: Establish relationships with local environmental organizations,

government agencies, academic institutions, and community groups. Recruiting and managing volunteers effectively will be key to your success.
- Ensure Legal Compliance: Understand and comply with local, state, and federal environmental regulations and wildlife protection laws. Obtaining necessary permits and licenses is crucial for your projects.
- Engage the Local Community: Develop outreach programs to educate and involve the local community. Public support and awareness are vital for the success and sustainability of conservation efforts.
- Implement and Manage Conservation Projects: With everything in place, start executing your conservation projects. This will involve coordinating teams, managing resources, and ensuring projects meet their objectives.
- Monitor, Evaluate, and Adapt: Continuously monitor the progress and impact of your projects. Evaluate the effectiveness of your strategies and be prepared to adapt your approach based on feedback and changing conditions.

Bringing it All Together: Discovering your Prosperous Path in a Transforming World

As we step off the beaten track and prepare to embark on a journey that we've uniquely crafted for you, remember the various alternative careers we've explored together, paths that don't necessarily require a traditional degree but which still hold great promise for a sustainable future.

These options, all fifteen, are an assortment of hand-picked careers, each possessing its own distinct charm and promising prospects. They demonstrate that having a fulfilling career is not solely confined to traditional degree paths. Your possibilities are just as diversified and abundant as your aspirations. Diving into digital marketing or becoming an arborist, learning the art of sommelier or venturing into renewable energy - the choices are myriad for those daring enough to deviate from the conventional.

Though challenging and scary it may seem to venture off the trodden path, remember the tales of those who trailblazer before you. Each nurturing their own skills, building their own foundations brick by brick, and invariably making a name in their chosen field without a traditional degree to their credit.

Anchor Your Journey with Action

Let's take these lessons and transform them from mere words on a page to stepping stones in your life's journey. It's about seeing the value in upskilling or undertaking an apprenticeship, finding a mentor, or joining a community of like-minded individuals. Consider which path resonates most with you and embark on learning more about it. Redefine your measures of success and take your first step towards a career that resonates with your soul, one that is both environmentally responsible and economically viable.

- Take responsibility for your future.
- Determine your core values.
- Implement the principles of Ikigai.
- Find your natural skills and passions beyond exam grades.
- Try a variety of personality tests.

Thrive in a Changing Economy

Bear in mind that this book serves only as your initial guide in this exploratory journey. To venture forth effectively and construct a fulfilling career, you'd need to dig deeper, delve into additional resources, commit to consistent learning, and never hesitate to ask for help.

Onward to a Bright and Sustainable Future

The world is changing, and as it twists and turns, so must our perceptions and aspirations. The security a degree once guaranteed us is waning. Instead, the world is turning towards skills, talents, and experiences that aren't always reflected in a piece of paper. The careers described in these pages are not limited within their definitions, but are a starting point for your imagination to take flight.

Allow this book to be your compass, guiding you into uncharted waters of alternative careers. Continue pursuing the thread of knowledge, unwinding more about the path that sparks your interest. Polish your skills, find mentors, and never shy away from challenges.

Remember, like a mighty oak that stands resilient against the storm, it is those who adapt to changes that thrive. Your future is not written in old-world rules, but instead, it's traced by the nimbleness of your dreams and the strength of your resolve.

> *"The future belongs to those who believe in the beauty of their dreams." - Eleanor Roosevelt*

Printed in Great Britain
by Amazon